TOKYO

POETRY

JOURNAL

Volume 10 · Summer 2020

Cover Art: New Dragon Painting シン・リュウズ (2018) 116.7cm×80.3cm. Watercolor and nihonga paint.

Send postal submissions & subscription payments to:

Tokyo Poetry Journal c/o Jordan Smith
Akabori Mansion 101, Yokoteramachi 10-1
Shinjuku-ku, Tokyo 162-0831 Japan

www.topojo.com
facebook.com/tokyopoetryjournal
soundcloud.com/youtube-topojo
Instagram: @tokyopoetry
Twitter: @poetrytokyo

CONTENTS

EDITORS' LETTER

It would not be amiss to say that writers—and poets in particular—are predisposed to thrive in seclusion. Most poems begin and end in solitude, in the elapse of a single mind thinking, imagining, dreaming. Only by being alone can we actually *will* things into a textual reality—by which I mean, slow the passing-by emotions and visions down to a stillness, so that we may look closely enough at them to really see them, see them so that we may ascribe language to them, creating the verses that come to be known as poetry.

Recently I was told that in order to write poems, one's internal world must always be wilder, more mysterious, and more thrilled with fascination than the external world. I suppose that is why I have found it incredibly difficult—even tiresome—to write in this past year. Poems hover as though a mirage, a memory. (As a poet friend hauntingly puts it: "I once, it seems, wrote poems.") The world, meanwhile, revolts and writhes and turns as if unable to sleep. What seemed previously a foundation has become a tunnel. I think many of us must feel very tired.

But even amidst this maelstrom of fever days which merge and diffuse, it is still poems that find me, teach me, turning walls into glass, windows bearing air; the air bearing what it always does, the many unsaid things. This milestone tenth volume of *Tokyo Poetry Journal* is full of work that draws on the abundances collected from a purposive silence—the silence of listening, the aloneness in which one commiserates with the sublime. They are poems that enact, give shape to, reckon with, and console the tempestuous and inscrutable external.

The poem is an architecture of spiritualities forced into physicality. Clouds forced into a box. The poem is the idea of home, forced into a house. Even in times in which writing seems impossible, when the internal world is delirious and at-once everywhere, I am comforted by the fact that there still remain poems. And they are unwritten, but they are patient. As Czesław Miłosz said, "There will be no other end of the world."

What do we do in the Year of Quarantine? Currently, Warehouse TERRADA is preparing an exhibition on poetry and architecture, the perfect response to times when creative language may be the best conceptual escape from our boxes, the most powerful way to will them from prisons into artworks.

Many have experienced this year as something horrifyingly new. For others, the trappings of pandemic were already de rigueur—and sometimes for decades. Witness Saihate Tahi's "Mask Poem" (from TPJ V4):

> I have this I wanna die, I wanna disappear,
> I only want to go to an aquarium feeling, and
> It's time to go walk around town. Christmas, illumination.
> The world seems to have nothing to do with me, such a bright, cheerful era.
> I should exist, though I feel like I don't.
> I'm walking, though I feel like I'm not.
> I have this I wanna die, I wanna disappear,
> I only want to go to an aquarium,
> Just for some bubblegum-like misery, for me, there is no need to die.
> Hiding my mouth, hiding my nose
> Just got to slip from the world's gaze
> In this easy suicide.

I wonder if it will be said someday that the urge to withdraw, to retreat into the easy suicide, is ultimately what saved Japan—the desire to find anonymity behind the accessory that has long been commonplace here: the hygienic mask. Could Japan's "lost decades" we wrote about in ToPoJo Volume 4 have been the unconscious rehearsal of 2020 social distancing?

I don't know. So much. It's a struggle to encompass a history even of the last six months. TPJ began quarantine with an online reading and then retreated into editing mode for this volume. Our editors did what many did. We don't even have to say it, because you already know. You did it too, in your own formula composed of some subset of the infinite variety of relationships between health, emotions, and economics. This volume pulls poetry out of all this. Puts poetry back into all this. Pulls us all out of this. Puts us all back into all this. Ignores all this. Obsesses over all this. Makes a home in all this. Seeks a home beyond all this.

That's why our poetry here begins with the life of God and ends with:

> Our eyes shut at our lightness, we are falling
> As if nothing had happened

But let's see what happens in between: time to read.

——by Xiao Yue Shan and Jordan A. Y. Smith

OSHIMA TAKEO
translated by Jordan A. Y. Smith

The Life of God

In my days as an actor
My agency was extremely powerful
They comped me a BMW, and I lived in a Minato Ward high-rise
Handed me a credit card with no max
which I used every night to gorge myself on fried and glazed sweet potatoes
However, I lacked acting talent
In my whole life, I appeared in just a single film
It was a love movie
set on a remote island
I played the role of a modern art critic
from the underworld
I embraced the heroine, a high-school girl
and whispered into her ear
"Good girls don't smoke"
That was the sum total of lines I ever spoke on screen—
Then I took an ice pick and stabbed the heroine through the heart
Her corpse was left to be eaten by the birds
according to the island's custom of "sky burials"
As I watched the birds peck her apart
I made a phone call to the heroine's lover
And begged him for some peanut crackers

I quit the agency due to an illness
It was an illness where each time I closed my eyes
I would see California, even though I'd never actually been there
The psych doctors couldn't discern the cause
and they referred me to a proctology unit
The proctologist was so kind and familiar
he went so far as to worry about my future
Even offered me his daughter in marriage
She's a great gal, none sweeter, he proclaimed convincingly
Her hobbies were reading train schedules
and collecting antique cameras
She excelled at open water swimming
He passionately urged, *Why dontcha take her on a date?*
Just as I began to think that not such a bad idea

my illness took a sudden turn for the worse
Almost simultaneously
the area around the hospital
opened up into a time hole
And the proctologist and his daughter
were blown off into the Cretaceous Period

Lacking means for self-support
I began to sell Sherlock Holmes
It ran entirely on commission
a business suited perfectly for me
I forgot about my flashy show biz life
and sweated as I walked around shouldering baskets filled with Holmes
Our marketing slogan was:
"A Holmes in every home!"
During the first month, I sold seventy-two Holmeses
and made top seller at the business
A year later, several districts were merged
and I was promoted to manager—
the outlook was splendid
However, once the town was saturated with Holmeses
the people we couldn't help started turning their Holmeses loose outside.
Abandoned in the wild
the Holmeses gradually began to wreak havoc on the ecosystem
Compared to the native variety of detectives
their reproductive rates higher
and their resistance to pollution was stronger
When the Ministry of the Environment
legally declared the Sherlock Holmes an invasive species
the company could do naught
but declare
bankruptcy

I sank into desperate and dilapidated circumstances
With nothing else to do
I opened up the laptop
and killed time watching classic pro-wrestling videos on YouTube
My concerned friends
found me a part-time job as the mayor of Tokyo
So three days a week
I went to the government offices and executed my duties
I repeatedly put my foot in my mouth and soon turned everyone around into an enemy
Year round, I was shot with machine guns

and I wandered the border between life and death
Eventually though, I got so used to it
that the bullets wouldn't even pierce my skin
From there, it dawned on me
to become a street performer
so I quit my job at City Hall and made my way to Ueno Park
I approached passersby
gave them guns and had them shoot me
With a peppy smile and a "Looky here—I'm still alive, aren't I?"
I collected spare change
But before long people became inured to the novelty
no longer thrilled by normal guns
It escalated into bazookas, mortars and anti-tank missiles
It became clear
that this would eventually become unsustainable
However, when small children in the crowd
stared at me and said
"Mister, show us more"
There was no way I could resist
using more extreme weapons
Finally, I started messing with ICBMs
then installed nuclear warheads
We joined voices for the countdowns
and I would let the cutest girl in the crowd push the button
Staring at the missile approaching me
I suddenly lost all motivation
I stopped the missile in my hands
ripped out the fuse, and declared
"I want to go back to being a normal guy"
I pushed my way through the dumbfounded crowd,
cut a B-line across the park
made my way over the Shinobazu Pond
And I chucked that missile right into the water

I sat by the pond clutching my knees, head hung low, when the Goddess appeared
She held a gold missile in her right hand, and a silver missile in her left
She asked me, *Which missile is the one you dropped?*
I replied, "Neither one—it was just a normal missile," and she grew fierce
What's going on in that head of yours?
Not even a gold missile, not even a silver missile sheepishly tossed
You simply chuck in a regular missile—what were you thinking?
Are you making fun of me?
The pond is not a garbage dump, you know.

Just as I was apologizing in earnest, the Goddess sank away once more
Then floated back up with her arms full of missiles
These are all the missiles that have been dumped into the pond
There are even some from the Nara Period
Since ancient times, Japanese people have lacked civic morals
I find even I am fed up
I had been putting up with it until now, but my patience is gone
I'm blowing them up, fuck it, I'm blowing them up on all you!
I tried to stop her, but too late
When it all ended, the Goddess and I stood in this world reduced to ruins

"Finally, the two of us can be alone," I remarked
"It's all your fault that things ended up like this," the Goddess replied, crying
"What's done is done," I offered, "So let's cooperate on a project for the future"
"Like what?"
"First, let's make a baby"
Instead of a reply, the Goddess slapped me across the face
As the sparks rained down, each spawned a love hotel
I kicked back at the Goddess, and her nose began to bleed
From that, beds and sheets were born
We traded an endless string of punches
Giving birth to room keys, automated pay stations
old ladies to work the lobbies and such
Neither of us could defeat the other
I'm a black belt in karate, but I couldn't get a single move past her fighting prowess
I staggered the Goddess with a reverse roundhouse
and a shrine for matchmaking was born
When the Goddess rocked me with an elbow strike to the chest
an amusement park and Ferris wheel were born
When I got the Goddess with a one-armed shoulder throw
the restaurant with the highest reputation on the internet was born
When the Goddess hit the ground and nimbly twisted straight into a sweeping leg throw
a white sand beach and twilight perfect where I'd confessed love was born
When the Goddess knocked my foot with her Achilles heel
the first hand I'd held was born
When I countered with a cross-knee lock
the pupils with which we'd exchanged first glance on that day we met were born
The Goddess escaped my cross-knee lock, stood, and declared
"I'm all out of techniques"
I was all out too, there was nothing left for us to do but embrace each other and kiss
And slowly but surely, we came to love each other
It was simply inevitable

From that point, we lived happily ever after
Marriages between parties of unequal social status are no good, the Goddess said
So I decided to be come God
The Goddess was kind and wise
Yet she had her psychologically unstable side too
She tended to rely on medicines
and if I took my eyes off her too long, she would overdose
Twice she lost consciousness and had to be carried off in an ambulance
Which, to be fair, is nothing more than a tiny hassle that could happen in any household
After she went through menopause, the Goddess's psychological instability waned
And her original kindness and consideration shone once more
A woman lovelier than she I've never seen
I know not how much more time together we will be allotted
But we cherish every second of every minute, to keep doing so our fervent wish
Lately there are days when the Goddess forgets who I am, starts thinking I'm a stranger
Frequently, she starts complaining, *I feel like money keeps getting lost around the house*
I myself have grown nearsighted, and can no longer read or write
This morning when I woke up, I'd soiled my underwear
But in our home, the smiles shine on
Because, for one reason or another, we love each other from the bottom of our hearts.
Ah yes, but there is just one thing that I've been hiding from the Goddess
It's something that happened during the Goddess second trip to the emergency room
When she was hospitalized for a while
The time hole opened up, and the proctologist and his daughter reappeared before me
He had made quite a fortune treating constipation in carnivorous dinosaurs
But he had worked himself to exhaustion, and could do little more than wait for death
He had bequeathed me his fortune, and pleaded, *Take good care of my daughter!*
On my authority as a God, I had built for her a high rise with metered parking lot
and set her up so she'd never have to work again
I left her the entire inheritance without so much as touching it
In honor of her father's profession, she christened the high rise and parking lot "Anal Castle"
and "Anal Parking," and she managed them both capably
And after years of laborious study, she too became a licensed physician and opened up an
"Anal Cosmetic Surgery Clinic"
My wife knew all about that though, so nothing to feel guilty about there
The thing I'd kept from the Goddess was that I'd been sharing a bed
with the girl once a month
And she had born us a daughter
There was absolutely no way I could reveal it
If the Goddess found out, I have no idea what she'd do, the world might even end again
So I kept our daughter hidden, and I raised her in the depths of Shinobazu Pond
Now she is radiant and beautiful, and is ruined by the complications
of being raised in such conditions, and has grown into a woman riddled with psychological

instability
If you ever go to Shinobazu Pond
Try throwing in a missile and see what happens
My daughter will likely float up, she'll ask you
Is the one you threw in the ruby missile or the sapphire missile?
And should you value your life as it is
You should respond courteously
Ruby and sapphire—don't be absurd! It was a diamond missile.
However, should you desire to lose everything
You should reply, *It was neither—just a regular missile.*
Declare it straightforwardly, just like that
If you possess such courage
My daughter will belong to you
And the world will belong to you
Your own burden to bear

MARCO HARNAM KAISTH

All Seasons

"The dead are together as pure souls."
—*Mei Yao Chen*

I

I have been in Japan 34 days when a man jumps onto the tracks
of my train. I am on the Tozai line from Nihonbashi towards
Nakano. I am closest to him, just across a set of doors. I see a
twitching arm pointing up, a narrow run of blood.

I am sorry for my indiscretions. For the people I do not keep in
touch with and for the things I wonder if they feel.

I wish to grow roses on the high central plains, to turn inward
and rust as lost tankers in the bay.
The dead are together as pure souls.
It is enough to be simple and to desire simple things.

II

The dead are together as pure souls.
Out in good winter, carrying that old joy
in each other's open places:
in each other's eyes and mouths,
in the little of their memories
where it (that old joy) clicks like brittle kindle.

The dead are together as pure souls.
I think we need new words and new fingers
with tight nails to pierce the skin of fat peaches,
to slint open the plastic wrap on those chicken hearts.
There's an easy joke here somewhere.
I wake up underground and say:
      "I'm alive! I can feel again!"
and laying there in the dark, bite my nails.

The dead are together as pure souls
turning over perfect cuticles they rise
and look at their gravestones broken down perfectly.

The dead are together as pure souls
smiling their own hands' webbing to ripe, blessed open.

The dead are together as pure souls
shuffling against us, here, against each other's nothing.
Carrying that old joy for us, carrying it on their backs
and under their fingernails, in the holes of their cheeks
outwards, like water, like winter filling open places.

The dead are together as pure souls
and they don't mind being porters, we've joked about it,
about getting them velvet doormen coats, gold-fringed fezzes.
        "You know,"
they say
        "we never really set us apart. I've visited the Artificial Life
        lab at Todai and know well the thesis that consciousness
        arises out of complex systems. But you are made of a hundred
        billion systems, and you make up a hundred billion more,
        many of which include us!"
so we break and talk about it (with hot chocolate),
our particles banging together. Our old
joy clacking together, like river rocks
drifting downstream.

The Construction of Simple Finite Groups

They spent too long on the crosses.
Each took at least three hours
to join, to smooth.

Digging out a posthole
to hold a 180-pound man
took another 30 minutes or so.

Would it have been easier
with just a sword in the gallery?
Well, yes, but then,

the next morning,
those first few shafts of light
would have had only some low hills
to shine on.

DURELL SMITH

Forbearance Come Warmth

Hell. Please let me enjoy this breeze
whispering summer and green. I
smelled the rain yesterday releasing dirt
from concave epiphany. Oh what life.
Sit with me. Overthrown petty
overheard dialects about ex-girlfriends
and the boys I enjoy the drone of rush
hour floating down eighty two. My feet
are sore sore. I'm not waiting for
anything anymore in warm month long
days. I'll take whatever hours I can and
spend them on nights none of throwing
myself into make or break or burst.

Simple joy. Simple joy. Simple summer
of no eminence. My pessimism is taking
a sojourn from decadent expectation. No
maps. I've fallen far from desired routine.
My memories are not to be built on. I've
let go of the burden of years gone. Moon.
Moon. Warm backpack midnight beer
carry me with you. May.
    July.
        June.

Maybe in the Pacific

I dreamt of you roaming
around Tokyo with your love
and cherry adorned
photographs hurled into the
ocean. Held under a blanket
while crying in my basement
would you ever consider a
melody again? Sold your
strings for better things we
rarely speak but sometimes
you crash into my mind. A
reminiscence of an old friend
while carried to work.

JASON SCUDERI

WE ARE ALL UPSIDE-DOWN

A photographic exploration of how COVID-19 has affected society, through a surreal lens.

While the coronavirus has drastically changed our understanding of modern day society, forcing the public and governmental bodies to deal with the pandemic in strikingly different ways with varied results, Japan has taken on a relatively slow lockdown process compared to the rest of the world.

This collection of photos derives from an archive of everyday strolls mainly throughout the Tokyo and Saitama prefectures. These images are an attempt to depict the slow infiltration of change by manipulating seemingly mundane scenes of various urban landscapes, violated by a sense of the uncanny with the addition of upside-down subjects going about their business.

UPSIDE-DOWN

WE ARE ALL

歩車分離式

・ふりかけ
田煮
乾物　デザート
小麦粉　8　缶詰
スープ　スープ
中華材料　9　カップラーメン
スナック　キャンディー
キャンディー　10　スナック菓子
11
リキュール　ウィスキー
新商品
CHILLED
お会計
本日限り
青森県産
つがるロマン
1790円
338

葬儀・法事・式場

EUGENE RYAN

Bullet train, Tokyo

Clotted silver burns,
neon hot,

elastic neuron pulse
across the wild
and febrile dark.

KEIJIRO SUGA

My Watermelon Days

I have found my retreat in the watermelon pavilion which is watermelon itself without decoration. What's so difficult is how you enter it because you can't make a hole on its surface otherwise you lose the juice. You think hard, you give up a lot, and it happens. Suddenly you are in there, perfectly protected from the world by watermelon juice which is vital, sweet, red, and highly energizing. In watermelon you are accustomed to sing Happy Birthday many times over and each singing becomes a dirge for a lost one. What is past. You actually remember a lot in watermelon because of the unsweetened sweet juice which is blood from the time when animals and plants were one. In watermelon your voice echoes and you feel you are a much better singer than you really are but nobody says anything snarky about it. By your singing the watermelon begins to vibrate and it causes other watermelons to vibrate, too. This is fun and it reminds you of Zorb that can be fatal if you go off the orbit but watermelon being so protective, no worries. For the rest of your life you might live in watermelon. "You dweller in the dark cabin, / To whom the watermelon is always purple, / Whose garden is wind and moon," (Wallace Stevens). "I can see fields of watermelons and the rivers that flow through them. There are many bridges in the piney woods and in the fields of watermelons." (Richard Brautigan). All this I write in watermelon with watermelon and for watermelon. How unimaginably sad is this. As *triste* as Tristessa in Trieste. My watermelon days have only just begun. Raise a watermelon.

LEAH ANN SULLIVAN

Notes from the COVID-19 Cocoon

t
h
i
s
h
o
u
r
a
d
a
y

the Nepalese clerk
tells me there are only seven deaths
I picture the skyline

a point for a smile—
I beat the cashier to her
have a nice day

the two photographers
in the park
stalk each other

empty café
outside the stadium
savoring the mustard…

deserted mall—
a young ballerina extends
her leg higher and higher

that deep breath that settles
heard of snow in Sapporo today
593 miles away

something about this moon
and the guy walking by
entice me to look up

new moon
rhododendrons pop out pink and white
from the blackest green

good vibrations
street azaleas dance beside
an idling refrigerator truck

it's been a long time—
May Day baskets left at neighbor's doors
how are they this year?

El Capitan screensaver
memory of tying the knot
on my old hiking boots

1.8 meters—
making room for the Holy Spirit
in a Kinko's store

ACOCHUA
translated by Jordan A. Y. Smith

pa•tic•spaghetti theme song

With all my heart, I pray
for tomorrow to be
    even more the same
to be yummier,
        plainer,
            and even more slothful in Love

With all my heart, I pray
for tomorrow to be
    even more the same
with a safer,
        cheaper
            and completely invisible Love

Today again: a soft something,
How many days of that very first scent,
Once,
    twice,
        thrice,
            and more:
            I want to savor it by the mouthful,
After all, in that time,
After all, in that time,
Life went waltzing on
If I opened my eyes,
Even this face would vanish

With all my heart, I pray this box will lock away
Another tomorrow-just-like-today,
Locked inside of today,
A truth
One-hundred floors underground

Round and round and round, retracing these steps
Please! Lock it away! Inside of today
What I want: a more frivolous love

Today again, an unknown someone
for how many days shall I consider this the first time
Tic toc tic toc pa tic toc memory be gone
After all, in that time,
After all, in that time,
Only in today can it be locked away
So even with my eyes open,
my face may remain invisible

With all my heart, I pray
for tomorrow to be even more the same
to be crazier,
        plainer,
            and even more slothful in Love

With all my heart, I pray
for tomorrow to be even more the same
with a safer,
        cheaper
           and completely invisible Love

Note: The pa•tic•spaghetti *theme song was part of the eponymous theatrical performance by the UNFINISHTABLE Theater Group in Tokyo 2020. This translation is independent of the rhythmic "free English" lyrics included in the song as performed on stage and recorded here with music by acochua and Codi.*

TODD SILVERSTEIN

Fugue

Catch-
come,
un coup de des?
jouez, monsieur?

comme d'habitude tempete

jamais
jamais
absorb
cancel
nullify

There is a tome whose
covenant is
fire
wherein: sky
      emerges
from the night
    philistines ride sand-
    scathed highways
red waters sigh & separate

justice ebbs and plays

I look in the mirror
(skin wrinkling to pus)
and I look in the mirror
(a nullified limb)

To be at the end of age,
ageless and weary,
heavy-jowled, deaf
to be constipated with
harmony
Kretschmar stuttered out
this curse
sick licks licking open
notes
putrid mouth pressing out
darting gray tongue
blistered mouth, broken
coherence
gasping mouth, grinning
with teeth

Fearful trifles! This villa
too neat—
You hear?
I am meister!
(must master the fugue)

And I look in the mirror
(slung out on dull hips)
flats
(fortelling scars)
sharps
(furious fifths)
reds
(flarings of cancer)

When the cup is hoisted
the dice are played
alighting on the albatross
bashing the boards that are
bones of the crew

in the pulsing of the storm as it
mounts
in god letting veil drop
from his eyes
in rogue cells, digesting,
expanding
in the ark's launch
in the rain.

The dice are played.
The dice are played—

Draw in sand soldiers.
Draw in slack miscreants.
Fair rows rhythm
(not yet riven into)
fair rows rhythm
(not yet soul stretching
threes)
fair rows rhythm
(not yet floundering, full of
fourths)
fair rows rhythm
(girt trampled, gut
trammeled, struggling
fifths)
crashing together
slammed to the crests
rhythm the wasted
harmony's drum

Jamais
The dice are played
Jamais plus
Rain surrounds the ark

You hear!
I am meister!
(must master the fugue)

Jamais
Jamais
The dice are played
the backwashing ship
as thrown bets scatter
crushing the ark

And I look in the mirror
(animate bone)
in the glass
(grimacing in silence)

Un coup de des
through pitch and yaw
the wood's seesaw
the poop's collapse
the captain's hands thrown
up
to shove the rudder
through his storm

Meanwhile at the villa
Haffner-Borghese:
a smell of burning
            still nothing to eat
a reek of sweat
the clink of a key
play
play
            listen…so hot
play
play

And I look in the mirror
(less than a hush)
in mirror's nothing:
nothing
no look outlives
reflection
not eye's plain
not the frame

Study the chosen:
their time in the tome
alone in the desert
sounding the tracts

At the villa:

       What, are you
wagging your tongues?
(Concise, crowning
conflagration)
Where is my dinner!?
       My reputation
Where is my meal?
       Slut fired my
dinner!
Fire the maid!
       Oh, fire the maid
Oh
       Where is my music
gone to roost
Imagine that day.
Rudolf acrowning in kingly
robes
Rudolf adorning worthless
florins
Rudolf, Rudolf

whole,
quartered,
eighthed,
diminishing
while lord,
inviolate,
hoards yeast
of miracles' bread

Puis, un coup de des
Shall we throw our lives
away?
The bets are laid
The dice are played
The captain's roll is come
"Sel" he thunders, whisks
off spray.
"Dieu," he whispers, "s'il
vous plais"

Le coup de des:
cubic, churning in the
water
eyes of black resolve
deep as a hangman's
gravity
flat white faces
of an effort or fate
plink plunk
splashing and crying
shuddering and spluttering
Jamais—
Jamais plus

The captain's head rolls up
above him, lightning
lacerated
sky
and each die's
inverted eye.

Oui, un coup de des
as if
as if
idea hits home
hand restores angular ark
clenching future in its fist
and letting line
a pallbearer

    Milk and honey are no
    promise of land
    nor suffering's reward
    nor breath of because
    they are what remains
    when remains are faith
    the presence of mountains
    dreaming of home.

And I look in the mirror
(born to old flesh)

Off with his head!
Oh
    Where is my music?
    Where is myself?

Fly through the villa:
Play
Play
    The bars rearrange
Play
Play
    A systole of pulse?

a vanquished curse
a surprise
a hope
a lazarus

And I look in the mirror
(scarcely able to speak)
open my mouth to the
mirror
say:
time is but a trap whose
chains we right
And I look in the mirror,
see the chasm
liminal
(built on reflection)

Morning brings friends to
the villa Borghese:
1: Meister, meister—we've
both of us come….
2: Look at this chaos! What
has he done!?

Un coup de des:
If that might, this will have
taken place
fragmenting fate,
annulling chance by
an act that defies
turning face to face
with vital eyes.

And I look in the mirror
say a chance, singular is
still a chance
(at a body I do not
comprehend, that cannot
comprehend me)
say form shall never be
seen before or again
say it is not rock,
not metal, not wind
not sky, not water, not
flesh, not death
undertaking neither buried
nor won
nothing that is past
and nothing that is not
come.

The fugue…the fugue and
the fall

1: Why, has he gone blind?
Can he not see?
2: Meister! Meister! God,
he's sick! Meister what ails
you?
A chair! A chair, quick!

honey
honey
home
home

The fugue
The fugue
The fugue

home

did I fall?

STEVEN KARL

Untitled Blue #9

& enough is enough is   not even nearly enough even   ever everyone one of even
ever & it is still   not nothing notable this work   this work to work out
work it out us of   anything anyone's anymore &   yea it is trying & by
trying it does anymore   to anyone to care & to   care & to no nah
can't can not this cancel   no cancel this their of   caring if even state state
even if mandates a state   of not-caring can't can not no   stop this caring if even
yea even if caring is   killing inside is killing inside   & little ones piled in
buggies in red hats   pushed along through pushing   along through another & children
so many children laugh   & still the cars come &   damn siren cars are everywhere
everywhere the damn   siren cars with the people the   people with the guns the
people with the guns on   highways the people with the   guns on dirt roads &
yea enough ever never   evidence enough & the gun   people itch & itch & oh the
ick of itch on trigger   fear it was said gun   people it was training it was
training that trained to   exterminate the fear & oh it   is not ever never enough
of the excuse & of   our fear what of our   fear of the gun people
faking unconvincing   accusations according to the   world of whatever bullet different
bullet difference bullet   difficult difficulty bullet with   differences do die mostly miserably
some medicine   meddlesome & yea yea   it is not enough to
go & write rage &   & the yellow hats laugh   & the children in the
buggies go by & bye   they laugh & inside some   dying & inside some fighting
some no dying yet yet those damn cars keep coming   & keep killing & us
escaping less & less us   for only so long before   bullet come done sung slashed
life lifed so so long   cause yea it enough is   enough not nothing but care
crushed same all same   but through fall day   children laugh no not dying
not today you will not   not you will have not   my death fist fight I
here here I am may   the children hold me to   the sky with their laughter—

Untitled Blue #12

                b b b   b b b   b b b   b b b
                 e e e   e e e   e e e   e e e
                  c   c c   c   c c   c   c c   c   c c
                   a   a a   a   a a   a   a a   a   a a
                u   u   u   u   u u   u   u   u   u   u   u
              s   s   s   s   s s   s   s   s   s   s   s
             e   e   e   e   e e   e   e   e   e   e   e
            w w w   w   w   t   w w w   o   o   o
              e   e   e   e   e h   e   e   e   u   t   t
               b   b   g   g   h e   b   d   a   r   h   h
                e   e   o   o   a h   e   i   r   c e
              l   l   r   t   d n l   d   e   h   r   r
            i   i   g   f   t e e i g   n   i   w   w
            e   e   e   a   o v e o   o   l   i   i
            v   v   d   t p e v t t   d   s   s
            e   e   o   & r   r   e   u   s   r   e   e
            d   d   u   l   e   s   d   n   a   e   t   d
             i   i   r   a   t   t   i   d   f   n   h   e
             n   n s   z   e   o   t   o   e w   e   s
             s   f e   y   n   p   w   n   e   w   p
             k   l l   h   d   s   o   e   r   i   i
             a   o v   a   t   b   u   e n   t
             t   w e   d   o   e   l   n   d   e
              e   e   s   u   b   t   d   e   o   t
                b   r   o   n   e r   m   v   w   h
                 o   s   n   h   h a   a   e s   e
                 a   &   f   e   e y k   r w g
                r   f   a   a   a i e   s   e a
               d   o   s   l   l   n a   a   r   r
               s   r   t   t   t g   d   f   e   d
               &   g   l   h   h t   i   e a   e
                t   i   o   y   y   h   f   l n
                h   v   v   h   w   e f   l   s
                r   e   e   e e   b e   t   w
                a   n   &   a   b   o r   h   e
                s   e   j   d   e d e   e   s
                h   s   u s   c   y   n   s   t
                m   s   n   a   c   a   a
                 e   k   m   e   m   r
                  t   f   e   e   v
                a   o   t   e
                      l   o   h
                       d   e
                        l
                        ie

K. V. TWAIN

Iriomotensis

The Iriomote wildcat (Prionailurus bengalensis iriomotensis) is a critically endangered species that lives exclusively on the Japanese island of Iriomote. The Japanese government is in the process of trying to make this island a UNESCO World Heritage Site—a move that concerns locals, who fear for the feline.

A cat is sleeping in the hollow of a tree...
She is stalking a lizard at the border of a dream.
She makes a quick assault,

                                        her body twitches in her sleep.
Later she dreams of a lesser great leaf-nosed bat[1] that gives her trouble.
It is a male that doesn't want to die,

                                  and gives resistance.
Her third dream is about her mother:

                immeasurable instants

                      of playing beneath the lights of fireflies,
                with the one who was killed on the road of destiny,
                    like others.
Her mother also dreamed about her mother.
Thousands of years of dreams are gathered in the species.
The cat is a luminocratic child dipped in the colors of the earth.
Time is stalking her,

                    with potent claws is getting ready to attack.
The steadfast cat doesn't want to die,

                                      and gives resistance.
Her fight will be a drawn-out affair or else a brief iridescent terror.

A skein of lilac light pierces the canopy and the cat's slumber.
The cat opens her eyes of infinite amber, scans the fairy-tale season.

History will speak of a cat that dreamed in a dying dialect.
A child will fall asleep, tired, and dream of the dreaming cat.

---

1 The lesser great leaf-nosed bat is a species of bat (family Hipposideridae) found on Iriomote and other Japanese islands.

SASA/MARIE
translated by Jordan A. Y. Smith

Inside My Ears

Inside my ears
where shadows flow

projecting dinosaur spines to drift up in the sky

I wake before the light of dawn
its white misty wisps disappearing
into sun-stabbed dream fragments,
the rising ripples nudging them toward me
'til they come to bob around my feet

On that distant shore,
you're standing,
calling out to me
who cannot hear your voice

drowning down
into the flowing water

What you're saying
somewhere beyond a quiet murmur filled deep with sadness
I've no way to grasp

In Japanese, to be able to hear is kikoeru
What happens when those letters
come to block the *ears* in *hears*?
Eru means *to get* or *obtain*, so can we not *get it* if we lack *eru*?
Can you get through hearing?
Or do the *gets*   get lost?
to get   not to get   to be unable to get   to where?

kiko   *kiko*   *kiko*

Sounds of a squeaky bicycle,
we stand on opposite shores
just staring across at each other

The words sculpted in your breath
reflect
dazzling bright scents all over the place,
scratching at the marginal voids
inside my ears

This is the degree of forbearance I've had to maintain

To cross the river, I've pulled the bank toward me
when crumb by crumb your voice
dropped out, I scooped it up

Under your wide open gaze
I held it up in full palms
and swallowed them whole
and faster than words themselves can express
I melted them in my hot sighs

Enough
with the onomatopoeia

So sway and sway and sway
the eyes of a snail
in that one midday

ALJAŽ KOPRIVNIKAR

To Rosa Luxemburg

To plant acacias in the desert
          To come and leave
To not say anything
          To grow up
Without fear of darkness
          To put on clothes
To use the mouth to speak
          To lower white curtains of tenderness
To not say anything
          To face the clouds
and to press lips

              On the Brussels sky
      On the Ljubljana sky   *On the Grožnjan sky*
    On the Prague sky   *On the Lisbon sky*
      On the Berlin sky   *On the Uppsala sky*
          On the sky

To glide before reality

With lips

              To tremble treble
    in the ear before sleep

GALE ACUFF

The Death of Me

I think I'm going to die. Miss Hooker
is my Sunday School teacher and she says
so, and that everybody must die
at one time or another, sooner or
later, and I think that about wraps it
up, my future, at least the last moment
but as for that remaining in between
I'd better get humping because, she says,
no one knows exactly when God will take
him. Or her. So if I die a sinner
that won't be good because I'll wake up dead
in Hell and wish that I could die better
if I could do it twice but it will be
too late for me. I'm only ten years old
and I really want to live forever
even if that means I'll miss my shot at
Heaven, living on with God and Jesus
and the Holy Ghost and all the angels
and all the good souls there. I might even
know some of them who got away from me
on earth, my dog and my grandparents,
the dead ones I mean. Father's father's still
alive and so is Mother's mother. They
could get married while they're still around down
here but I guess I'm missing the point, I
do that a lot, which is why I'm failing
third grade but there's always next year, unless
I'm dead of course. Which means no more homework
and no more memorizing poetry
so it can't be all bad. No more playground
fights. No more terrible lunchroom lunches.
No more smelly school bus. Instead I'll have
wings, that is if I rate Heaven when I
kick. Miss Hooker says I must stop sinning.
No, Gale, she says—*no one lives forever,*
you can't count on avoiding God that way.

The Final Judgement, she means, after I
croak and my soul is released like a belch
out of a bullfrog and floats up to God
and stands somehow, if a belch has legs, in
front of Him. He'll look in the Book of Life
and if I'm not in it then I'll be damned
but I won't be surprised. Then He'll toss me
into the Lake of Everlasting Fire,
or at least that's another version of
the story. It's bad enough not knowing
what to do when you're alive—I don't know
just what happens afterward, either, meet
God or Satan? I'd ask Miss Hooker but
every time I raise my hand she says
God moves in mysterious ways, so I
don't even bother to offer. I ask
my folks but they say, *That's why we send you
to church.* Last night I took it to the Lord
in prayer, right after I said *Bless
Mother and Father, my friends, and my dog,*
who's still dead, and the Lord's Prayer, which is
easy to remember, I'm glad that I
can do something Jesus can, it gives me
confidence. *O Lord*, I said, when all that
other stuff was out of the way, *Why do
you make saving my eternal soul such
a pain?* Then I fell asleep and when I
woke it was Sunday morning, like always,
so I got dressed and ate and went to catch
the legendary catfish in the pond
behind the cemetery below our
church. I didn't get him but I think I
saw him. If it was English class he'd be
a symbol. I'd have to write a paper.

CARL WALSH

Niseko miso

The cloudiness of my miso is reflected in afternoon sky with dark seaweed stretches of *kombu* cloud and strips of white tofu. But this sky is perforated with tips of stratovolcanoes. Active in their inactivity—they may surprise at any moment—3,000 years just a nap. I wonder how old I am in volcano years? My head hurts at the maths. Perhaps I should

get Isabelle to calculate it. Some consider a volcano active for 10,000 years, dormant after. But even dormant ones are prone to throwing unexpected parties. I glance at Mt. Yotei, its dark bulk everywhere I look. I hope it's content with its sleeping. That *Kagu-tsuchi-no-kami*, the fire-spirit, is happy. I stir my miso—and the clouds burst with rain.

NORA KIRKHAM

Morning Crows

They clipped a clothing hanger to their nest
outside our home, white hooks stitched
between twigs and missing things.

They stole a bundle of soft toast in a
napkin thrown across our neighbor's roof.
Butter shimmered on their wings.

In a trance I watched them perched
on the edge of a branch, as they dropped
bread and worms into loud, pink mouths.

They flew where we could not follow,
clawing the sky between the city's towers.
I hear their caws echo in the early hours.

Before I rest my legs on the family bed,
I might open a window, hear them lifting
their dark bodies. I might lose them.

MICHELLE EGAN

Mountain of Souls

Japanese itako *were traditionally blind girls who learned the craft of spirit communication:
how to command nature, cure the sick, and educate the crowds who gathered to consult them.
Mount Ozore, in Aomori prefecture, has been their home for centuries.*

Itako-san's shrill rhythmic laments
(for *itako* trill their unspoken chants)
are broken snatches of incantations
that ring through my ears perhaps salutations.
Improvised songs filled with composite rules.
A clutching hand shakes beads to heal wounds.
Kneeling before her approach the bereaved:
a lover, a mother, those who are grieved.
Itako-san swiftly snatches for pains,
evoking solutions from alternative planes.

*

Itako-san with a hallowed face,
transporting anguish into a place
of comfort, of joy, of images bountiful.
Sharing a moment in awe insurmountable
when poised in your tent, sweltering love,
surrounded by desolate fissures above
on the hillside leading down to a lake
whose sulphurous shore gives respite to heartache.
Glowing white sand where undead linger on,
offerings stark left to those who are gone,
sadness resting in pungent air.

*

In a temple, priests are kneeling for prayer,
beating a drum to uplift and empower.
Crows watch over each fading hour.
Banners creak; beneath, pinwheels whirl.
Life at its darkest gives cause to return.

HIRATA TOSHIKO
translated by Eric E. Hyett and Spencer Thurlow

Is It April?

I've been thinking about the poet Shuntaro Tanikawa
today
yesterday
the day before.
On Sundays, the library wears
a tired face.
I take out three books
by Shuntaro Tanikawa.

I'd always meant to go
to the bus stop cafe,
but they demolished it.
Next door, Osugi Medical Partners
is still in good condition, a place
I still might go someday.
I guess a clinic
lives longer than a coffee shop.

I read Tanikawa.
I write a little about Tanikawa
try an essay, end up
writing line-break poetry.
My body invaded
by Tanikawa's rhythm.

Day before yesterday,
I saw Shuntaro Tanikawa from afar.
I heard Shuntaro Tanikawa speak.
Getting old can make you go on and on,
never give up the mic
like you're holding onto this world.
Tanikawa's speech was crisp, fun and light.
Tanikawa seemed far-from-old.

Someone I'd always wanted to meet
died last month,

which doesn't mean that the people I don't want to meet
live forever. Chiyo Uno, author of *I Will Go On
Living*, died.
And someday, Shuntaro Tanikawa too.
Everyone will raise their hands
to write the eulogies.
But the one I most want to read
is the one Tanikawa himself would write:
crisp, fun and light.

In seven minutes, today will also end.
A day with no likes, dislikes,
nothing good, nothing bad.
Today
Yesterday
The day before.
Today, yesterday, the day before.
Sunday turns to Monday and I'm still not done
with Shuntaro Tanikawa.

Is It June?

Last night, someone came to my door
whispering *Can I stay?*
Breathless, I let him in
double-locked the door
behind us.

He was sweating,
shivering through a white shirt.
I set out
cold drinks
hot drinks
and he took the cold
in one gulp
collapsed on the bed.

I'd been waiting for the day
when he'd kill someone,
whisper *Hide me*
I'd protect him with my life.
I chose this in my heart years ago,
never moved,
never changed my number.

As always,
he slept with glasses on,
as always,
hiccupped in the night.
I watched his face sleeping
beneath the fluidity
of years.

Next morning, he had not awoken.
Evening, still asleep.
How can anyone sleep
so soundly
after killing?

His face was so peaceful, he'd even stopped breathing.

I'd been waiting for the day
when I'd offer his last rites.
For his sake, I never killed myself.
Even if I'd been hit by a car, I would not have died.
I poured one last glass,
wet his lips,
finished the rest myself.
I stroked the hollow of his cheek
like a line from an old movie:
Whatever happens, my darling, I'll never let you go.

Is It July Again?

I get a phone call from a friend.
She wants me to wake her up at 7 A.M.,
because she knows I don't sleep.
It's for something important, she said.
Seems simple enough,
but as soon as I tell myself
just don't fall asleep
my eyelids droop.
The hours that always seem to disappear
have come to a dead stop tonight.
I have a feeling I won't be able to stay up until morning,
so I call a different friend:
I've got something important tomorrow
so could you wake me at 6:55 A.M.?
She likely felt her eyelids droop, too,
called someone else,
Can you wake me up tomorrow at 6:50 A.M.?
A vicious cycle
making its rounds
like a circulator bus
through my circulatory system
(how boring!)

I want the wake-up call for my friend
to be a song, sort of a *Morning Call*.
Flipping through the pages of *Beloved Musical Classics:*
Mozart's *Lullaby*
Brahms's *Lullaby*
Schubert's *Lullaby*
music that only puts you to sleep:
a trap sprung open when *The Cuckoo Bird Song*
suddenly appears.
It's been a month since my last encounter
with a cuckoo bird.
This time, the cuckoo
is a song by W. T. Wrighton, translated

into Japanese by Sakuto Kondo
in the early 1900s.

I know this song
from high school music class,
Miss Matsuyama played it on the piano.
We were allowed to sing it only once
before she moved us right along
to *Santa Lucia*.
I guess *The Cuckoo Bird Song*
didn't have great educational value
(although it's a good song)
I sing *The Cuckoo Bird Song* over
and over,
trying to recall the parts I got wrong   in high school
It's well past seven in the morning
and I still can't stop singing.

Is It August Again?

There was this word, *biddy*,
in a book I borrowed from a friend
years ago.
I had always overlooked *biddy*
even though I'd read the book
countless times.

What is a *biddy*?
Someone who bids   on horses?
An itty-bitty person?
According to the dictionary,
a more matronly, common-sense definition than I'd expected:
"an old maid who does laundry."

In those days, *laundry* meant
rinsing cloth and cotton in water.
no machine, no suds.
Imagine the biddy from the Peach Boy fairytale
picking peaches
on her way back from the river,
discovering the mythical Peach Boy
as a reward for her eco-friendly lifestyle.

Are there any biddies alive today?

It could have been the old lady I passed yesterday
but her clothes smelled like laundry detergent,
which disqualified her.
Also, the dog she was walking
didn't look like it would enjoy
being washed.

Today's biddy, also no biddy.
Her grandson's clothes, instantly dirty,
no matter how much she washes.
She loves too much

the long moment
when she helps the little boy take off
his dirty clothes.

As for the lady I saw two days ago
she was no biddy either,
walking her shadow, which was shrunk in places
where she didn't wash it right.

At this point, biddy
only exists in an old dictionary.
Nothing left to wash except
her glass eyeball,
her dentures.
Just washing all day
in an old dictionary.

Is It September Again?

A friend of mine (let's call him Mr. X)
is performing live at a bar near Nishi-Ogikubo station.
He has quit his job,
will soon be moving to Osaka.
I don't know why he's moving away.
He himself might not know.

Usually, Mr. X wears a drab necktie
and glasses.
But today, he's wearing a flashy T-shirt.
Who knew Mr. X had a day look and a night look?
Does he have a dawn look and a dusk look?
He hollers into the mic
alternating between two guitars as he plays.
I chain-smoke ginger ale in silence,
feeling awkward, as I thought I'd known him.

Thirteen years ago,
I moved from Osaka   to Tokyo.
Back then, Nishi-Ogikubo was my station,
and my apartment, a fifteen-minute walk.
The more I walked, the longer the road seemed to get.
My landlady was an elegant, sophisticated older woman.
Each month, when I handed over my rent,
she gave me the sense that I was really,
truly living in Tokyo.

When I was in that apartment   on weekday afternoons
I'd hear someone turn the key in the entryway lock.
The door would open,
my landlady would step in.
Pardon me, she'd say,
I didn't know you were home, then leave.
My Osaka landlord would have never
come into my apartment uninvited.

Did my landlady even know
what she came into my apartment for?
I hadn't known why I moved to Tokyo,
but maybe she did.

After Mr. X's show,
I thought I'd buy a book at True Love Books, on Shinmeidori Avenue
to commemorate my return to the old neighborhood.
It's on the first floor now,
since they turned that building into brand-new condos.
I look for a copy of *Treasures of the Dharma*
but can't find it.
I settle on *The Joy of Bondage.*
Aren't they close enough?
Isn't S&M
Buddhism's night look?

Is It October Again?

I can still smell the sweet olive tree.

No warning signs a day earlier,
but when I opened the window
on the first of October,
I smelled sweet olive wherever I went.
It was like the trapped fragrance
was let loose, lifted,
swirled around me.

The day my cat got hit by a car,
thirteen autumns ago,
also smelled of sweet olive
Since then   I get sad every year at the smell.
This year the smell was lovely.
Does this mean
I'm starting to forget her?
Her body, pure white—
each time I saw a white cat, I thought
Is that her?
I used to see her in every white bag.
I used to see her in every white pillow.
I had to force myself
to say *that's not my cat*,
but I'm not doing that so much
anymore.

On Mount Fear,
the ground is white like scattered bones.
The smell is hot sulfur
springs trickling from summit
to ground,
dry ground mottled yellow,
water gone.

The shrine at Mount Fear is a quiet place,

only one oracle,
so there's a line in the shrine corridor.
Four women, no longer young,
wait their turn, sit sideways.
I join them, sideways and silent.
The oracle, inaudible
on the other side of the glass.

I hear some people are visited
by their fathers' living spirits.
If so, why not a dead cat?
Is she willing to take form?
To come back?
Could I take her home,
if only for us to catch up,
enjoy sweet olive
together.

POLCHATE (JAM) KRAPRAYOON

Cassandra, a Meditation on the Possibility of Romantic Love During the Anthropocene

So no one wants to hear: "I told you so"
I know it's hard for you to see ahead
while I just look behind, as time extends

before it circles back to you and I.
It's clear that this was a bad idea, you
and I, society at large perhaps,

with its black smoke and endless tired squares.
It's hard to see the fraying shapes of things
and how or when they'll fall apart. We're cursed

to have an urge to look beyond the veil
and watch the curves slope down below the lines
on graphs with names like *'Climate Change Effects…'*

So why did I decide to swim across
 that gap between our lonely little beds?
I knew I'd drown inside of you, your eyes

in mine, as waters rise and swallow us
in whole. But fate's a funny string
that's spun by gods and other ancient things

into our minds, and prophecy is just
that nagging itch you get behind your neck
that lies and tells you that this must be it.

CYNTHIA ABDALLAH

Ulale ngoxolo Madiba

Of leopard skins, slaughtered oxen, swollen feet and body aches
Of Zulu dances, siyabongas and enchanting hallelujahs.

of

    heavy   hailstones

    night   sweats

           crescent

    moon   shines

    tall trees   thick leaves

         bats

    hanging   upside down

DAH

Fragment No. 7

With you, I remember, without
wasting thoughts: and for us, at
the root of strain, the staggering
distress: gesticulations, like frag
—ments of perjured love: for
nothing ever came as answers.
What have we done? A thous
—and formless feelings. Lost in
swift detachment: at risk of be
—ing stressed. And you, both of
us, on the side of spasms: twist
—ing, coiling. My own hard insu
—lation, like some iron winter.
Burning. Shivering. Pushed und
—er ice. Chilled to the bone. Dis
—harmonic, cracked at the center.

From 1952–54 the Japanese director Kenji Mizoguchi was awarded
the second best film award (The Silver Lion) at the Venice Film
Festival for his films *Saikaku Ichidai Onna, Ugetsu Monogatari*, and
Sanshô Dayû. They are all period dramas; the first two are set in
the 17th century and the third in the 11th century. The role of women
in Japanese society is placed at the dramatic forefront. *Saikaku Ichidai
Onna* is one of the greatest feminist films in all of cinema: its chronicling
of a woman's suffering and destiny is heartbreakingly intense. *Ugetsu
Monogatari* portrays a wife of a potter who is killed in a terrible civil
war—inside this 'war' film is a poignant ghost story. Whilst *Sansho
Dayu* concerns a princess and her two children who are kidnapped,
sold into slavery, and kept in a brutal work camp. The film's tragic
ending has been compared to Shakespeare, and the critical reputation of
these works is huge. They are regarded as amongst the greatest films
ever made. Although themes, ideas, and a Buddhist-like philosophy
overlap, Mizoguchi didn't intend them to be viewed as a trilogy. But
for the challenge of writing prose poems to convey their imagery, I've
grouped them as a sequence under the title *Prostitute, Peasant, and
Princess*. And because Mizoguchi's art creates such an epiphany, I've
inserted my own personal reaction to his films, re-worked as poems.

———Alan Price

ALAN PRICE

Prostitute, Peasant, and Princess

(1) SAIKAKU ICHIDAI ONNA (The Life Of Oharu), 1952

Her used body refutes men's status yet accepts
its own sweat. All the crouching, swerving, running,
stumbling and falling cannot break or save her now.
Oharu's brief pleasure is not theirs; slipping down
from courtesan to concubine, shopkeeper, prostitute
then labelled 'goblin cat'. The wife of a lord watches
his concubine view a puppet show. Sold into a court
of desire for an offspring. Oharu won't be bought
as she sires a son that's pulled from her arms.
Slapped like a fish on a chopping board she flops,
despising law and order. When old they rent her
a gaudy dress and underwear but Oharu returns
to claw and hiss. Each movement of Ohura's hand,
touching her veil, cries out disdain, holding intact
a huge sad grace. They'll not abuse what's deepened
inside. She fainted inside me, shaming us all
for our looking on. I retreated from the screen.

(2) UGETSU MONOGATARI (Tales of the Watery Moon), 1953

Sunlight, enchantment, erotic truces and Lady Wakasa
appear as a potter brings his merchandise to the market,
over-reaching for a dream bigger than his family.
A deceased princess lambent in a ruined house
tempts her man and artisan to love firm and long.
Ambition, money, delusion and a civil war reside
as a mother with child, tied to her back, is struck
by a spear to totter on the path, made cruel and tender
for all to view. Miyaki reappears to sew her husband's
kimono; become a domestic ghost united with Genjuro
who will now create pots more beautiful than before
when he lost his soul to the kiln, greed keeping its fire
alight. Once I watched my mother mend a pair of trousers
and argue with father till each forgiving stitch was outed.
Now Mizoguchi's camera tracks down all evil spirits
intent on destroying fired earthenware and any belief
in the humility of sewing.

(3) SANSHO DAYU (Sansho the Bailiff), 1954

Zu-shio An-ju, Zu-shio An-ju, Zu-shio An-ju, Zu-shio An-
Cry of an aristocratic woman spanning time and space.
Why were Tamaki and her children sold into slavery?
Wrenched apart, dispatched to torments: sold for a legend.
Her wail turned into a song composed of loss, fire and water
learnt by a weaver in the camp, invoking the memory
and heart of sister and brother. *Zu-shio An-ju, Zu-shio An-ju*
Names as telepathy cutting deep into birdsong woods,
escaping through a gate, rippling on the lake of the drowned,
capturing that most cruel of stewards, angering the state,
inciting rebellion and demanding freedom for all slaves.
A parallel fate was the savage breaking of Tamaki's tendon,
her blindness, chanting and collection of mute seaweed:
asking to be banished by the embrace of mother and son.
And a mythic song be silenced by father's mercy, both real
and mystical, approaching the edge of the seashore. It hurts
to see characters in a story suffer too much. I wanted to
rescue this family from a life of beautiful compositions.

JOY WALLER

How to Be a Human

Ask your body.

Let your body be a pendulum that sways you to the left or right.

Divorce your legs from your mind, only for an instant, and see if they start walking to the
east, down Dogenzaka and through the crowds and daytime neon to Shibuya station, where
you can take a train to anywhere in Tokyo, or if they start walking to the west, through the
quiet residential streets of Shinsen.

Observe your feet as they take you there. Notice if you're wearing high heels or Doc Martens
or flip-flops. Make note of the pavement below you, the steps and escalators, the grass. These
are clues as to who you are and where you're going.

Ask your body what it wants inside itself. Ask if it wants coffee or tobacco or salad or
somebody else's tongue. Respond accordingly. Set plans in motion. Reach for your purse or
your fridge or your phone. Keep asking and listening, in case the order changes. Alter course
if you need to. Practice saying Yes. Practice saying No. Practice smiling. Practice caring.

Make sure you have one place that's all your own. Pick Atami, a coastal resort town
30 minutes outside of Tokyo that was popular with newlyweds 50 years ago. Take the
Shinkansen out there and spend a couple nights at a hot spring hotel whenever things get to
be too much. Soak in the onsen at least four times a day. Walk around the beach by yourself.
Go make-up-free. Buy oranges and scones at the Seijo-Ishii supermarket and eat them alone
in your room. Make lists for self-improvement. Delete numbers from your phone. Go back to
Tokyo with waves and seagulls and clear skies in your head instead of tension. Smile at other
people on the train.

Choose your intoxicants wisely. Avoid marijuana because it increases your anxiety. Avoid
cocaine because it makes you mean. Purchase MDMA regularly, from Nobu-san or from
Chevy, and dose intelligently, monitor your serotonin levels, bliss out. Do acid on Sundays, if
the weather's nice and flowers are in bloom. Try on and off different lenses. Appreciate the
different qualities of sunlight in your experience, the different shades of shadow cast by the
trees and benches and rose bushes in the park.

Ask your body if there's anything you can get for it. Determine if it wants a massage, a tattoo,
an orgasm. Listen to your body when these things are obtained. It speaks in sensations rather

than words, so try to get still enough to feel them. Listen for uncertainty, for pleasure, for boredom. Listen to feedback, positive or negative. Learn to cherish the neutral. Hold onto it like a just-warm-enough coat.

Take your body out to interact with other bodies. Do this regularly. Cultivate a lover who is not too close and not too far, and drive with him to rivers and restaurants and love hotels. Hold hands only when you are having sex. Make breakfast and coffee for him in the mornings, if he has spent the night, and do not think of him at other times.

Nurture friendships with people who align with certain interests. Label them the Techno Friends, the Tarot Friends, the Poetry Friends. Do techno and Tarot and poetry with them. Assemble Work Friends, as well. Go to lunch with them on Wednesdays at the Thai place by the office. Complain about your schedules. Send them funny pictures of cats.

Synchronize your lifestyle with the phases of the moon. Initiate creative projects on the New Moon; host or attend parties on the Full Moon. Intensify and soften your activity levels when she waxes and wanes, respectively. Ignore the negative press about Mercury Retrograde and spend these periods reflecting, re-evaluating, and removing. Note how your menstrual cycle links up with the different moon phases. Take the train to Enoshima by yourself at night, and lie on your back on the cold beach, shivering as the tide in front of you, and the tide inside of you, crashes in, and whispers out.

Ask your body if it has ever been another body before. Research your Pleiadian origins, if any. Meditate on your breath, moving in and out of you, and keeping you alive, and ask yourself why you consider it your breath, when it seems to come from somewhere external. Do the same thing with your heartbeat, your blood. Settle into the rhythms of biology. Stop asking questions and just feel.

Spring Visions: Tokyo 2020

Glimpses of eyes
        above masks

Invariably startled-looking,
      sexy

The streets of Tokyo
infused with masked
gods and goddesses

Disguised

Free, suddenly,
in our anonymity

Eye contact
      much more
           prevalent

People hold
     a gaze
        longer

Hands hang
     uselessly
     safely
        at our sides

It's a different kind
     of touching

Tokyo, Japan
April 2020

CHAY CANCERAN

02: in a dance

dance like no one's watching like
a dance that no one watches a
dance that no one likes watching
no one dances like no one's
watching there is always one who
watches like a dance where
watching is like a dance: No.
one's watching.

MICHAEL FRAZIER

In Response to "The way you write about Black death is cliché."

a low coup

sorry
that my lack
of creativity
keeps killing
the puns, metaphors
unique ways
our bodies die.

In Response to "What takes you so long to reply to my messages?"
a low coup

                                                    guess how long

                                                    I've left God

                                                    on seen.

                                                    You lucky

                                                    I'm alive.

Eastern Standard Time; Japan Standard Time

mom
   wakes before her alarm does   upright, she stares   into the loosening dark   now the
comforter   reaching for the floor   the bathroom light   faucet   turned   the burn
of warm water   winter skin   towel   tight above breasts   arthritis stiff scrubs   coffee overwhelmed
into notcoffee   anymore   door   obscured sunlight   the keys   the keys then back outdoors her
breath   visible   in the car   the heater   low hum   Siri says   *I don't recognize that name*   Ma' says
how? Mikey   my boy   redial   the phone rings until road   erodes into parking lot   the windows
fogged   she rolls   them down

lets the silence out.

JOHN SOLT

untitled

all these trinkets
don't mean anything
when you've lost
your mind

custards
in the swimming pool

JEFFREY JOHNSON

The Coronation

of origin in no place or time
mythical and legendary
no scent, no sound
no symptom except psychopathy
invisible, irresistible
immune compromised
in the great compromise

ring around the rosy
blistering fever
the providence of locusts, lice, rodents
towns empty
stores shuttered
the dead in heaps in hallways
of the great infirmary

reaper on the road
to nowhere
headless horseback
haunted dreams
and days alike
touch your cheek
at your own peril

on the pinnacle and the precipice
tottering for a fall
the fall in a tangle of sweaty sheets
the hallowed eve
is come early
child's play
a disguise of RNA

don your masks
and chemical amulets
no one comes back
to tell about it
to tell how the Crown fits
how it feels
in time for the scourge

hear the cock's crow
take the long walk
to the mount
where you'll be framed
in the line of your ancestors
who wait for your arrival
in the burial carriage

born of a bat
as in legend
castle-dwelling
black-cape-draped
turn-of-the-century
decadent dandy
spewing offspring

little black-winged mammal
the creature strikes
sensual fear
its promise
of life eternal
carries the demise
in its own Crown

TAYLOR MIGNON

Top Ten of Japanese Poetry:
after the Nanao Sakaki poem "Top Ten of American Poetry"

I am a burning meditation, I hold a watery island inside.
—Shiraishi Kazuko
私は燃えるような瞑想をしています。中には水の島があります。
白石かずこ

Don't light my fire.
—Otoboke Beaver
ドントライトマイファイヤ
おとぼけビ〜バ〜

Throw away your books and hit the streets.
—Terayama Shuji
書を捨てよ、町へ出よう。
寺山修司

In this world we walk on the roof of hell gazing at flowers.
—Kobayashi Issa
世の中は地獄の上の花見かな
小林一茶

Never trust the marathon man who walks in a straight line.
—Torii Shōzō
まっすぐに歩くマラソン男を信用しないで
鳥居昌三

Out of the back of a girl applying makeup zebra-style, an antenna juts.
—Tsuji Setsuko
化粧ゼブラスタイルをする少女の背中から、アンテナが突き出る
辻節子

To stay young, to save the world, break the mirror.
—Nanao Sakaki
若さを続ける、世界を救う[すくう]ために、鏡を破る
ナナオサカキ

I would love to offer you even something as tiny as a grain of sand.
—Hijikata Tatsumi
一粒[ひとつぶ]の砂のような小さなものでさえも提供[ていきょう]したいと思います。
土方巽

The current of the flowing river does not cease, and yet the water is not the same.
—Kamo no Chōmei
流れる川の流れは止まりませんが、それでも水は同じではありません。
鴨長明

Art is my life and my life is art.
—Yoko Ono

TAYLOR MIGNON

The Value of Poetry in the Time of Emergency

During these times of upheaval, poetic and artistic composition becomes—for the most part—more recognized, encouraged, and vital. While this poetic impulse resonates strongly, the resulting texts may or may not be unique; there is always the risk of succumbing to cliché, didacticism, populism, or social network-inspired preaching-to-the-choir inclinations (as the humanizing effects of common experience may soften our critical cognizance). What is—or should be—the role(s) of poetry in times of war or devastation? Must poetry instigate social change, or is it merely a practice of escape from reality, a form of self-expression, a self-initiated therapy, a manner of meditation, an activity to keep one busy as one aims for a kind of catharsis? Is it one way of taking control while chaos reigns? All may apply; in the case of the pure poet, one doesn't compose with preconceptions or an agenda.

Early in the Kamakura period, Kamo no Chōmei wrote the famous poetic personal essay 随筆 *zuihitsu*), *Hōjōki: The Ten Foot Square Hut*. Arriving amidst an era of natural disaster, devastating earthquakes, tornadoes, mass fire, and famine, this masterpiece (taught in schools throughout Japan) is a spiritually deepening read, engaging in its encouragement of perspective and wisdom. It is the kind of text that one selects for company when setting off on a long trip, and could arguably be considered a pioneering self-help book. "The current of the flowing river does not cease, and yet the water is not the same water as before," (translated by Yasuhiko Moriguchi and David Jenkins) has become a dictum. In this case, the horrifying circumstances of the 1200s instigated a brilliant classic.

In most cases, however, poets rarely succeed in creating works that are neither pedantic nor trite, though certain figures who have excelled in polemical poetry come to mind: Kenneth Patchen, Kenneth Rexroth ("Thou Shall Not Kill"), Shiraishi Kazuko, Yosano Akiko ("Thou Shalt Not Die"), Nanao Sakaki ("Anyday," "Let's Eat Stars"), Allen Ginsberg, the war haiku of Saito Sanki, and TPJ matriarch Barbara Summerhawk ("Unraveling Richard"). The particular events we experience may provoke thought and determine the grist of poetry, but the best works have enhanced the reader's appreciation of life without necessarily making a practical change in society. Perhaps the change poetry can instill happens gradually, rippling into the future until transformation is attained. Of course, when artists attempt to directly reply to a political or destructive event, the resulting work is often predictable, and only serves to raise certain shudders of disgust as one is further reminded of the catastrophe. Therefore, poetry which approaches its subject askance often acquits itself with greater grace than the political poet shouting from the pulpit.

BARBARA ROETHER & TAYLOR MIGNON

Pandemic with Crows & Crowds

Sound glib? Hammock therapy epic in pandemic
or pandemonium with a secret agent
s/he it refuses to sing dance cry DJ or go away
so we mimic its threat, collisions of crows in the noon sky
they quickly congregate, throwing shadow on pavement
dark in umber chatter then the dinner crowd at dusk
dissembles & disperses into dumberfound metro neurotic hermits
we are all masked bandits knowing we'll never get away

JEFFREY JOHNSON, TAYLOR MIGNON, BARBARA SUMMERHAWK

T(aylor)P(arpara)J(effrey) in Collaboration

Silent spring night; supermoon rises coughing
wheezing in the breeze

Petals fall,
bringing down the house
of cards

cherry blossom petal blizzard—hold the cliché—ah! refreshing earthquake

peachy keen fever, tu-lips at a distance, quivering...

Spring steps
A Blizzard of Quakers
In a Red dawn

Urawa Lotte chocolate factories, Cedar Rapids Quaker Oats: Crunch Berries

Stocks fall
into winter
no coins left for laundry;
sundried desert
dateline

Deadline, headline
Where's John Prine?
Lonely tee shirt spins round

Unlikely bedbabes, The Normal Prime Mover Deadheads ineffuckable jam

break out, go viral, dance on my preset grave; atone...
scratch your way out of a premature grave, the coronation and fingers to the bone
1/4 baked geniuses Adderall mad: word-croutons of improv Caesar

HACHIKAI MIMI
translated by Kyoko Yoshida

Now

A flounder is thick as an unleafable book
A smell of sand creeps to mingle
with the silence carpeting everything
Islands and continents furiously alter their silhouettes
and cross past each other   exuberantly

A departed person's piece of clothing
hung out in the sun   to dry   flutters
more eloquently than its late owner,
proffering   lights and shadows
(some things cannot be undone)

After the border between the sky and the sea
slips   into the field of vision,
only meanings are washed up ashore

A body has neither inside nor outside—
its cells continue to dissolve and reproduce,
carrying   the moment of silent eruption
so as not to spill over,
until a human shape takes place
here and now
and—
eyeing how thick a flounder is,
we cross past each other outside its field of vision

Sweet

A herd of emotions is led as effortlessly as a herd of sheep
You step forward   among them
Before you know it,   the shadow at your feet is tinged with lies
Nudged,   pushed,   and swallowed,
This scene, makes you wonder

Right by the side of the roof over my head
At night there is a tree that bears fruits
It dangles fruits with such greed that its branches break
Any single one is every bit overripe
    Spitting-pit
        Overripe—
            Playing strange music tapping the roof
        The tree has a beehive
    During bright hours,   diligent buzzes
Slip in and weave through
Onto the transparent ceiling
Buzzing fingertips slither
Once satisfied, they take off
Coaxed
Not by words   but by wind

(A colossal silence catches up)

Homo sapiens sapiens
After two-hundred thousand years from the beginning
A silent lid is put over this pandemonium
Kind faced, do we melt each other
Down to one being, into one cerebrum?
<You must be qualified to mourn>
We forget such cases might happen
And react and release
In exchange of being everywhere
Being nowhere, we are supported by shadows
Rationed to   each   one   of   us
Which reveal our posts

Unquestionably like flags
Yet veiled
To some

(A colossal silence in the shape of a receptacle)

Scenes pour in through our eyes and remain at the bottom of our bodies
There, and yet untouchable by fingertips
They become   domesticated   presently   fiercely
Overripe—
Once orphaned fingers
Peeled the skin of a fruitlike thing
Time runs   through the valleys   of fingerprints
Out of a few fruits remaining on the branches
Confessions are extracted and they loosen their orifice
To release lustrous pits onto the earth (strange music)

Hold on to the present fingers
The fingers are tangible
They make up a living part
Of others, for instance
(Apoptosis)
And an example of solution
That would respond calmly   to be part of
The gazed scene where
Death is designed in advance

Lying on the soiled earth
Licking up
A quiet train of ants
We are licking it up
The train of ants remains quiet
Sweet—
Our dimensioned judgment half-baked
Our eyes shut at our lightness, we are falling
As if nothing had happened

RYO MICHICO

translated by Hana Pivinskaya & Mideki Fernando

Excerpt from *What Overflowed Was Kindness*

From a reflective essay about the poetry writing workshops she taught at the Nara Juvenile Prison; her project was also the subject of a BBC Radio 4 program titled Rewriting Humanity.

One poem, consisting of just a single line, instantly opened the doors to everyone's hearts:

Cloud

The sky is blue, so I chose white.

My knee-jerk reaction was at the line's sheer poetic power. The agent behind the sentence—the identity behind the "I"—is elided, waiting to be revealed by the title. The poet is speaking in first-person from the perspective of a cloud, "The sky is blue so I chose to be the color white and float in the sky."

I asked the young poet (referred to here as "D") to please read it out loud.

Gazing at the floor the entire time, D read through it with a halting yet frenetic lilt. It was so unclear that I wasn't sure what I was hearing.

At the time, D was suffering from the long-term effects of drug addiction—including a speech impediment. His head bore a painful scar that his father left after hitting him with a metal bat—that may have also contributed to his speech issue. Due to the abuse, his parents' rejection, and his lack of confidence, his gaze was fixed constantly on the floor. Perhaps his rapid speech was an attempt to shorten the length of time he had to speak, even if only by a little.

"I'm sorry, I couldn't quite hear you. Would you mind reading it again?" I coaxed. Yet I still couldn't make out his words completely. It was such a short poem, I kept encouraging him to read it once more. "Sorry, you'll have to look up and read more slowly so your classmates can hear you better."

D finally looked up and spoke clearly enough for us to hear, "The sky is… blue, so… I chose white…"

His friends looked relieved as they listened with bated breath, then burst into applause.

The supervisor and I applauded too. Every face in the room beamed with happiness. The applause, truly heartfelt, had no obligatory note to it. Then, D shyly raised his hand and said, "T-teacher, um… I, have something I want to say. Is that okay?"

I was shocked; he'd gone from slumped over and barely speaking to taking initiative and asking permission to speak further. That was the moment the door to his spirit opened up.

"Of course, please go ahead."

D began to speak. Those few words of his have lingered in my heart to this day:

"Today marks seven years since my mother's death."

I felt a lump in my throat. D's story, which came out in fits and starts, went something like this: *My mother was weak. But my father used to hit her all the time. I was still just a little kid, so I couldn't do anything to protect her. Before she passed away in the hospital, she told me, 'When things get tough, look up at the sky. I will definitely be there.' I wrote this poem thinking about her, imagining her point of view.*

I was overwhelmed, struggling to hold back tears—such a deep story behind this single line of poetry.

D's words opened the door for the other students attending the lecture as well. One after another, their hands popped up.

"I think that just by writing this poem, D showed us what a loyal son he is."

What kindness! D's sense of guilt about not being able to protect his mother from his father's violence was palpable. His classmates sought to reassure him—*It's okay, you're a great son. That poem you wrote was like a memorial for her.* But as a matter of fact, this boy had been imprisoned for a grave crime: murder. How could such a sweet boy wind up in such a situation?

Another boy raised his hand.

"It made me think that D's mother must be so pure that she was as white as a cloud."

My mind could not piece it together. *Why would a boy like you, with such immense creativity, end up committing a crime with no thought to the consequences?* But I swallowed my words.

"Me too! I imagined that D's mother having this soft, billowing kindness, like a cloud."

Compassion carried the day. One question ran through my mind: "Why on earth did you end up in this prison?"

Then one hand shot up into the air. "Go ahead, E," I said. Even though I had called on him, E had a hard time speaking. He was tall, but he always hid his height, hunching over into himself. He too always looked down and typically wore a sullen expression. It seemed so dark around him, as though he was being followed by a spotlight of gloom.

He struggled to speak: "I… I… I am…"

A giant, invisible wall seemed to be blocking his way. E was desperately climbing it. After a while, he finally managed to speak:

"I don't know my mom. But, after reading this poem, I started to feel like I can see her if I look up at the sky."

I burst into tears. Everyone in the classroom began to comfort him.

"I had no idea!"

"You must've been so lonely!"

"You're so strong!"

"I never met my mom either."

Through all these words of encouragement and sympathy flowing from his classmates, E wept. The supervisor too was bawling.

That day was a dramatic turning point for E. Until then, he had been compulsively self-harming, but it suddenly and completely stopped.

E was so horrified by the severity of his own crimes that he had repeatedly attempted to end his life, convinced that it had no value. Each time he did, he was locked in solitary confinement. Perhaps that day, for the first time in his life, he was able to openly admit the loneliness of not knowing his mother. The experience of having all his peers accept his truth must have healed his heart.

The next month when we held class again, E was unrecognizable. He looked noticeably taller. His slouch had disappeared, and he stretched now to his full height. In the last class, he was all smiles, and was interacting with everyone.

There is an epilogue to E's story. After the end of the half-year social reintegration program, we visiting instructors could no longer meet the students. However, I had the opportunity to meet E one more time when he was interviewed for a TV news program.

E, whom I'd last seen half a year earlier, was radiant. His improved posture made him look like an entirely different person.

"I was made a deputy leader in the training field!" he beamed proudly.

E, who used to be something of a burden on others, had become the deputy leader—what a transformation! But what he said next startled me so much I nearly fell out of my chair.

"Lately, I've been listening to a lot of other people's problems."

I nearly burst out laughing. I felt assured that he would be fine, that he'd been successfully socially rehabilitated, as they say.

People can understand the suffering of others if they too have suffered deeply. That's what made him such a great listener. The past cannot be altered. But how one lives in the present can change the meaning of past events. In other words—the past can be altered.

At that moment, the room began to sway. "I feel dizzy," muttered the supervisor.

"You're not just feeling dizzy—the building is shaking!" E replied.

I looked out of the window to see the treetops of the poplar trees along on the edge of the playground swaying. Large, slow movements, like underwater plants. It was the Great East Japan Earthquake.

Shortly after, the news showed the inmates the full extent of the earthquake's damage. I wonder how they felt, watching the endlessly repeating footage of the tsunami.

When I met them again in the classroom a few weeks after the earthquake, they were all shocked.

"It's so frustrating to be in jail—there's nothing we can do to help."

"Out there, the survivors are suffering so much, while we're getting three square meals every day—makes me feel guilty."

One after another, they expressed similar thoughts. Society may hold the stereotypical belief that criminals just pass their time in prison without a care, but that's far from the case. Each of them, in their own way, was deeply concerned about the victims of the disaster. The more I got to know them, the more I saw exactly how skewed the monstrous stereotypes are.

RICHARD MILNER

A Phantom of Atomic Light

Yamaguchi Tsutomu, And the River Flowed as a Raft of Corpses. *Translated and edited by Chad Diehl. New York: Excogitating Over Coffee Publishing. 2010.*

Reading *And the River Flowed as a Raft of Corpses* feels less like flipping through the pages of a collection of poetry, and more like what every great book aspires to be: an inhabitation. It is a vibrant composition, a breathing, in-the-moment reliving that tethers together a past and present that most of us, blessedly, will never have. It is an invitation to partake in a life that wishes its poetry was not necessary, but also warns that it may yet be.

Written by dual-survivor (*niju hibakusha*) of both the Hiroshima and Nagasaki bombings, Yamaguchi Tsutomu, and translated by Chad Diehl, *And the River Flowed* recounts Tsutomu-san's firsthand experience of not only living through both atomic bombings, but grappling with the trauma for the remaining sixty years of his life. Tsutomu-san lived most of his life, chronologically, after the bombings, but—in his own words—fears he died on those days. In his late years, he describes himself as pressed between the worlds of the living and the dead, waiting for the death he felt had happened sixty years prior.

The collection consists of around fifty poems, and is split into three main sections: "Trauma," "Remembrance," and "A Personal Matter." The first section recounts the events of the bombing and their immediate aftermath as experienced firsthand by Tsutomu-san. The second section is more or less a response to the first and acts as a call to activism, or a general meditation on the need for peace. The third section is a retrospective on the imprint that the events of those days left on Tsutomu's life and family. Diehl organized the structure like this, chronologically, and in so transformed Tsutomu-san's standalone tanka (traditionally metered poems) into a narrative with a clear through line. The effect is heart wrenching and brutal in its effectiveness, especially as it depicts the slow crawl of Tsutomu-san's final years with imagery, sentiments, and pain, signposting his passing in 2010.

In fact, this collection is so intimate and profound that it's almost embarrassing to suggest that anyone has the right to hold it up to critical scrutiny. Everyone's trauma is different, it's true, but this poetry was birthed from an experience that has to be, objectively, one of the most horrific that anyone could undergo. From the white of human fat carried along the surface of water, to the scent of burned flesh and cracked torsos split open and unrecognizable, this poetry is replete with savage imagery. The compressed, terse but flowing, and unrepentantly honest descriptions are absolutely purposeful, however—by necessity they call attention to not just the horror of events, but the need to absolutely ensure that such hell does not occur again.

Of course, the horror of the bombings and their very real effects on the lives of individuals—and our subsequent awareness—could not be so deftly drawn were it not for the skill of the writer and translator. Diehl has done a tremendous job heading up this project and bringing Tsutomu's work to an English-language audience. The introduction to the collection, artfully written by Diehl and immensely reverent, explains not only how the project shaped up but also some of the challenges he faced when translating the meter and syllabic structure of Tsu-tomu-san's poetry into English. It's extremely informative, and an invaluable tool for gaining further insight into the technical prowess needed for English speakers to be able to access this work.

In the end it's fairest to say that the earnest desire of the team behind *And the River Flowed as a Raft of Corpses* to bring Tsutomu-san's works to the world has been duly matched by the talent needed to do so. The grasp meets the reach, and the result is the creation of a confessional work that memorializes the life of an individual as brave as he was tormented. Tsutomu-san's words rightfully sacralize the lessons of the Hiroshima and Nagasaki bombings, and erect in their place a monument to the passing of the dead and an entreaty to the living for a final, lasting peace.

DAVID COZY

Floating Transit Center

Meg Eden, Drowning in the Floating World. *Winston-Salem: Press 53. 2020.*
Keijiro Suga, Transit Blues. *Canberra: Recent Work Press. 2019.*
Yoko Danno, Further Center: Poems 1970–1988. *Kobe: Ikuta Press. 2019.*

Meg Eden is a poet who writes in her first language—English—often about Japan. Keijiro Suga is a poet who writes mostly in his first language, Japanese, about different places, and translates his Japanese poems into English. Yoko Danno is a Japanese poet who writes about different places as well, but directly in English. These three poets, therefore, offer a catalog of different relations to language and subject.

The poems in Eden's *Drowning in the Floating World* are the most explicitly topical. The majority were written in response to what has come to be called "the triple disaster": the earthquake and tsunami that hit Tohoku, and the subsequent meltdowns at the Fukushima Daiichi nuclear plant. As is, perhaps, appropriate for material that was news less than a decade ago, many of her poems could be described as poetic reportage: portraits of people, places, and things affected by the disaster.

News gets old, though, and the old is forgotten. Eden's purpose seems to be to pour the bad news from Tohoku into vessels that will endure, to add them to a lost and found like the one in "Rikuzentakata," a poem named for a town in Iwate almost completely destroyed by the tsunami:

> Outside the town hall, a lost
> & found for the dead: shopping
> baskets filled with photo albums
> & a wall lined with children's red
> backpacks, still full.

One sees Eden's strengths here, the eye for telling images, the willingness to evoke them simply and let them do their work. Simplicity, though, cuts both ways. If Eden's goal is to lodge those horrible days in memory, perhaps poems less forthright, poems that force us to read and think, reread and rethink would have been more effective.

There's no shortage of that kind of fruitful complexity in the poems collected in Keijiro Suga's *Transit Blues*. Take, for example, the opening stanzas of the long title poem, the centerpiece of the collection:

> Transit. I'm in transit.
> Sitting in a train that doesn't even run.
> Like a hobo *sin rumbo*. Without direction.
>
> Transition. My perception is in transition.
> My position on the ghost train in the sky
> Is a juxtaposition of my forgotten past and my foretold future.
>
> 'The blues has always been a migratory music' (Charles Keil),
> Your position and transposition urge translation.
> Translations occur as proofs of distance.
> A migrant's song can only be the blues.
> Singing the blues in the bluest lights of Yokohama, California.

The notion of transit is invoked at the beginning, and move we do, on a train and on a ghost train, on a train that is still but flies through the sky, through time, through transit, transition, and translation. We hear the scholar Charles Keil on blues and migration, and finish the third stanza with a different musical blue, the blue light of Yokohama (but also California). There is a density here that rewards, and the music of the verse makes it dance: the bounce of "a hobo *sin rumbo*," the rhythm in lines like "Your position and transposition urge translation," the words that don't rhyme, but carom off of each other: position, transposition, transit, translation…

The poems collected in *Transit Blues* were first published between 2012 and 2018, so it's not surprising that Suga, too, if more obliquely than Eden, also reacts to the triple disaster. One of the vehicles he uses is the animals left behind. He writes about cows abandoned post-meltdown (as does Eden) but also gives us a dog who "…tries to connect somebody breathing and somebody blinking / And make them talk using unknown words." This gives us a sense not only of the desolation of the region, but also the thoughts of a canine loping through it, thoughts as incomprehensible as those of Wittgenstein's lion.

And he gives us ravens silently watching:

> …beings travelling on the shore.
> They are numberless, but neither a group nor a flock,
> One by one, one by one,
> They cross the cold water,
> Being washed by the beautiful light

Pouring down from between the dark clouds.

For a poem about a tragedy to leave us with sadness and anger might be a kind of success; for a poem about a tragedy to leave us with wonder and awe is something greater.

Wonder and awe are our constant companions as we move through Yoko Danno's *Further Center: Poems 1970–1988*. The awe comes in part because it's hard to see how poems so spare can leave us so pleasantly stunned. Many of the poems from "winter journey," for example, limit themselves to just twenty or so words spread over fourteen or so lines arranged into six or so stanzas. There is often, in these poems, a twist in the tail:

> the glazed
> ground
> began to thaw
>
> she looked
> back
>
> to shake
> the dew
> from her straight hair:
>
> the pointed
> trees
> stood leafless against
>
> the slippery
> sky
>
> like a triumph

"Triumph" surprises, and that Danno succeeds in springing this subtle surprise is just one example of her skill with the language she has chosen for her poetry. Many of the poems collected in *Further Center*, far from being direct reactions to the news, are instead reportage from the deep time of mythology and prehistory. Paradoxically, though, because the myths and history Danno draws on continue to underlie the news through which we are moving, they remain relevant. She writes, for example, of

> an invisible shadow
>   creeping on the land
>   like secret ink
>
> we have no time to lose—

storehouses burnt
the crops blighted
dust storms creep across the roads
to the shrinking
             lake.

The poem was published in the 70s, but she could have been writing about the aftermath of the nuclear meltdown in Fukushima. The fact that she's not writing about that disaster, or any other disaster in particular, gives her poem greater resonance than it would have if more narrowly focused.

The almost thirty years' worth of poetic work contained in this volume delights in countless ways. There are arresting images: "the owl-hooting forest," clouds that "crumple / to a / drop / of water," a tree that grows "from / the / scene / of / green / carnage." There is the mastery with which she organizes groups of poems, as in the section "dusty mirror" where each poem is connected with the one that follows it by the repetition of the last word of one poem in the first line of the next.

The only part of the book that seems less successful is the final section, a prose poetry fantasia in memory of Danno's son, who died in a mountain climbing accident. For all the emotional power of this section, it is, perhaps, a bit too raw. One misses the cool eye and disciplined language of the earlier sections, though it's not hard to understand why Danno chose to veer away from those qualities given the nature of the topic.

This final section is but a small part of a book that is a major achievement by a poet who boasts one of the most compelling voices of any of our contemporaries. One wonders if, as with Beckett and Conrad, writing in a language that is not her first makes Danno a better writer than she would otherwise have been. It is undeniable, though, that Danno, Eden, and Suga are all stronger poets for the borders they have crossed, the walls they have vaulted.

XIAO YUE SHAN

By the Nature of Things

Kiriu Minashita, Sonic Peace. *Translated by Eric E. Hyett and Spencer Thurlow. Dallas: Phoneme Media. 2017.*

It has always seemed strange to me that in literature—and poetry specifically—there is a concurrent invasion of novelty: the desire to write that which has *never been written before.* A marvelously absurd idea, considering that neither words, nor anything we apply them to, can be new. Everything has been written before, just as it all has been seen, has been felt before. I do not say this despairingly, but with wonder.

Newness in poetics has a peculiar manifestation; originality does not result from the poet's expressed creation, but reimagination. She treads the distance between the word and the infinity it conjures and contains. If the word has any value—if, indeed, it has *meaning*—the poet does not discover it, but elects it to perform, in function and fascination, a role that acknowledges both its origin and its newfound realities. It is not that the object itself changes, but that the light shining upon it does, allowing the affectation of newness. The word is not invented. It becomes light. It is a testament to the poet's artistry that in this evocation, we may find in the paths of visioning—not something new—but a knowledge of qualities, enduring. The power of the poem lies within its certainty that nothing begins nor ends with the word, the line, or the language.

Kiriu Minashita's sole English-language collection, *Sonic Peace,* is a slim volume of poems whose contents betray their limits to stray towards the outbounding nature of the earth. Each poem is smitten in conjugation with terrene elements—the moon, the rain, the dawn—that so often appear in verse, but Minashita's poetic gifts are not to scrutinize their presence, but rather the significance of what we have named them.

> The streetcar moon dwells on your shoulder
> slushing and crawling through sky.
> Leaves tinged with metal odor
> shelter the liquid horizon.

The pervasion of nature in these poems is not as backdrop to the goings-on of human life, but as an active and energetic agent in the formation and extensions of our experiences. The moon *lives* on the shoulder, *moves* across the sky. In brief lines and restrained description, Minashita rejects the idea of the landscape as a stationary object, aptly laid out for perception; she urges back into our awareness the incessant activity and interaction between us and the natural world.

In the afterword, she muses on the transformative quality of words: most notably, what is lost "at the moment when the generative force of nature is converted into a natural force that can be calculated." The word, in its promises of definition, cages its subject. One is reminded of those heart-wrenching lines of Robert Hass: "Or the other notion that, / because there is in this world no one thing / to which the bramble of *blackberry* corresponds, / a word is elegy to what it signifies."

In Minashita's poetics of rethinking, she isolates the word from symbolism, summoning instead its sonic or visual qualities, rescuing the meaning from oppression, restoring nature's "generative force". If the word is rinsed of its signification, it is then free of abstraction, relieved of its innate struggle of encapsulating the unsayable; it does not beckon towards the infinite, but becomes a part of its stream. In the Japanese language, Minashita accomplishes this by wrenching the word out of its accustomed writing system—writing a word normally denoted in kanji or hiragana into katakana. The translators of *Sonic Peace*, Eric E. Hyett and Spencer Thurlow, should be commended for finding a graceful—though of course, not perfect—solution of how to replicate this linguistic simplicity into English: the visual disruption of a dot.

生存スルモノハ
生存スルハズノナイモノ

Whatever survives
de•fi•nite•ly should not have survived.

In this disturbance, we are forced to prioritize the word's sonic qualities, reinforcing that idea, beautifully iterated by Eduard Hanslick, of music as the purest art, because "in music there is no content as opposed to form, because music has no form other than the content". By reintroducing form and content to one another within the small scape of a single word—in which the two are antithetical—Minashita insists us towards harmony.

In George Steiner's essay "Silence and the Poet", he remarks on three directions of poetry's transcendence: towards light, music, and silence. I have spoken of light and music, and now I would like to say something about silence.

What unites the disparate and proliferating texts of contemporary poetry is essentially an impassioned and contradictory distrust of language. Writing poetry today is an act of both political and personal assertion, an acknowledgment that words are not merely representatives, but complex modules of intersecting narratives that grow with etymological, contextual, and cultural applications. There's a certain comedy in it—that the great romance transpiring between poets and language is one of intensive, ongoing investigation and negotiation: the oftentimes painful, oftentimes compromising attempts to harvest from the word a truth that measures up to the absolute truth of wordlessness. The revolutionary statement of *Sonic Peace* is that nature is, by itself, writing poetry, and so perhaps has no need for poets, and their ineffectual, human language.

First published in 2005, *Sonic Peace* arrived in a world that was still struggling to come to terms with the precise ravage human beings have made upon our planet. Though the now-buzzy neologism "Anthropocene" had already been coined, it was not yet a term most people were willing to face. The Kyoto Protocol had just been put into effect that very year, but climate change deniers were occupying significant platforms (as they still do today), and environmentalists were largely undermined by a savage simplification of their cause. *An Inconvenient Truth* was still a year away. By 2017, however, when the collection arrived in English translation, the facts of human-led environmental degradation were painful, terrifying, and no longer detractable. The consequences of this damage have progressed even further since, becoming ever more damning. So it is that reading *Sonic Peace* today, in Japan, Minashita's verse is both prescient and harrowing.

> I was born
> with mass-produced hopes
> a mass-produced life story
> dumped over a mass of dead bodies

Yet this is a volume that reflects upon itself as "a love story", and it is by the means of tenderness that Minashita pulls us back into the body, and into the profound realization of an innate tragedy: that the destruction of the world is not only a deprivation of the only place in which love may occur, but also the only way we have to love. It is all the emotions driven by earthly things like rain, summertime, animal bones, the voices of crows, that inform the sacred way we reach out for one another, desire one another, and know ourselves.

The doorway into the world of *Sonic Peace* is there in its title: listening. And listening specifies a unique requirement that other sensualities do not: the quiet. Quietude is not only a suppression of our clamoring egos, it is also an expression of supreme generosity. It is the recognition that the world, and its time, does not belong solely to us. That the gifts we have received are ever more numerous than that which we are able to give. It is why we reserve moments of silence for deep gratitude, commemoration, and experiences of the sacred. Such silences are not to focus on inner monologues, or to organize our thoughts; hidden within their depth is the promise that if you surrender your conceit, if you listen, you will be rewarded with something beautiful.

> And so,
> on this earth
>
> forever
>
> wherever
>
> I kept listening—
>
> fragrant sunlight　　fragrant sunlight
> fragrant sunlight　　fragrant sunlight.

TEN YEARS OF TPJ

COLLAGES BY INKA PIIRONEN

リアルで

In reality.

切り取られた時間が

Time is torn up

風で散らばっていく

*And scattered
on the wind*

蓮の茶を
すすれば
悟りの微かな香気

Sipping
lotus flower tea--
a slight fragrance of enlightenment.

Void
mind
seasonless
like a bomb shelter
like a space station
no leaves changing color
no cherry blossoms falling

BIOS

Cynthia Abdallah is an emerging Kenyan writer. She has recently published a poetry chapbook titled *My Six Little Fears*, currently available from Amazon. She also writes short stories, and is keen on releasing a collection soon. You can read her work at missabdallah.com.

acochua gathers the world's idle and useless. Direct inheritor of the blood of her mother, who likes to freak people out, and her father with his bizarre finger dexterity, she is the spoiled youngest of three sisters. In 2010, she founded and served as frontman for the musical unit "spoon+", then founded the musical theater performance unit "Unwwww-finishtable" (Mikansei-na shokutaku) in 2020, for which she produces totalized performances integrating a variety of visual technology. With performance as her homebase, she serves as a director and art director for music videos, MC, video model, and so many other things that no one really knows what she's doing anymore.

Gale Acuff has had poetry published in *Ascent, Chiron Review, McNeese Review, Adirondack Review, Weber, Florida Review, South Carolina Review, Carolina Quarterly, Arkansas Review, Poem, South Dakota Review*, and many other journals. He has authored three books of poetry: *Buffalo Nickel* (BrickHouse Press, 2004), *The Weight of the World* (BrickHouse, 2006), and *The Story of My Lives* (BrickHouse, 2008).

Chay Canceran was a Creative Writing and Literature teacher in the Philippines. She has independently published two poetry collections, *Certain Everythings* and *Eventual Goodbyes*. Currently, she is residing in Kita City, Tokyo, working on an independent project called *tokyo in verses*.

David Cozy is a writer and critic. He edits the Reviews section at *Kyoto Journal* and is currently self-quarantining on Japan's Shonan coast.

DAH's ninth poetry collection is *SPHERICAL* (Argotist Press, 2019) and his poems have been published by editors from over a dozen countries. He is a Pushcart nominee, Best Of The Net nominee, and lead editor for the poetry critique group, The Lounge. DAH is working on his tenth poetry collection. His eighth book is *Full Life In The Day Of A Poet: Selected Poems* (Cyberwit Publishing, 2019).

Michelle Egan is from the UK and has taught English since 2005. She spent six years in Tokyo, and is working on a collection of short stories and a novel set in rural England.

Michael Frazier is a poet and teacher based in Kanazawa, Japan. He received his BA from NYU, where he was the 2017 poet commencement speaker and a co-champion of CUPSI. His poems appear, or are forthcoming, in *COUNTERCLOCK, Construction, Visible Poetry Project, Day One*, and elsewhere. His writing has been supported by Callaloo and a Brooklyn Poets Fellowship. Currently, he's a staff reader for *The Adroit Journal* and a 2020 Seventh Wave Editorial Resident.

Hachikai Mimi 蜂飼耳 is a poet, novelist, essayist, and translator born in Kanagawa in 1974. She has been awarded the Nakahara Chūya Prize for *The Quickening Field* (いまにもうるおっていく陣地), the Ministry of Education's Fine Arts Award for New Writers for *The Night the Eaters Are Eaten* (食うものは食われる夜), and the Ayukawa Nobuo Prize for *Some Water to Wash My Face* (顔をあらう水). She has published novels including *Red Crystal* (紅水晶) and *Turnover* (転身), as well as essay and review collections such as *The Stone that Pulls in the Sky* (空を引き寄せる石) and *Cho-May-Yomi: Hachikai Mimi Books Reviews* (朝毎読: 蜂飼耳書評集). Her translation of classics such as Hojo-ki (方丈記) and Tales of Tsutsumi Chūnagon (堤中納言物語) have been received with critical acclaim. She teaches creative writing at Rikkyo University.

Hirata Toshiko 平田俊子 is one of the most notable contemporary Japanese poets. She has published more than ten collections of poetry, including her 1984 first collection *Spring Onions Return the Favour* 『ラッキョウの恩返し』 and her 1997 Banzai Prize winning *Terminal*『ターミナル』, which was awarded the twelfth annual Hagiwara Sakutaro prize in 2004. Hirata also writes novels, plays, and essays.

Eric Hyett is a poet, writer, and translator from Brookline, Massachusetts, USA. Eric serves on the Board of Brookline Interactive Group, and teaches a memoir class for parents living in public housing. Eric's poetry appears in magazines and journals, recently *The Worcester Review, Cincinnati Review, Barrow Street, The Hudson Review,* and *Harvard Review Online*.

Jeffrey Johnson did his doctoral work at UW Seattle and teaches comparative literature and translation in Tokyo. He is the author of two books of criticism: *Boakhtinian Theory in Japanese Studies* (Mellen) and *Haiku Poetics in 20th Century Avant-Garde Poetry* (Lexington), and is a founding editor of the *Tokyo Poetry Journal*.

Marco Harnam Kaisth is a poet, artist, and researcher based in Tokyo and Chicago. His work has been featured in publications including *E ratio* and *Another Chicago*, and he has exhibited in the Zimmerli Museum and *Commiserate*. He is currently a Global Leadership Fellow at Waseda University. Find more of his work at mhk.dev.

Steven Karl is the author of two full-length collections of poetry, *Dork Swagger* (2013) and *Sister* (Noemi Press, 2016), and is Editor-in-Chief for the online poetry journal *Sink Review*. Born in Philadelphia, PA, he currently lives in Tokyo and teaches creative writing and academic writing at Waseda University. Links to recent publications can be found at stevenkarlpoet.wordpress.com.

Nora Kirkham is a writer based in Scotland and raised in Tokyo. She holds an MA in Creative Writing from University College Cork in Ireland, and is currently pursuing an M.Lit. in Theology and the Arts. Her poetry and short stories have been published in *Ruminate Magazine, Bacopa Literary Review, Rock & Sling,* and *Topology Magazine*, among others.

Aljaž Koprivnikar (1987) is a poet and literary critic. His poetry debut *Anatomy* was published in 2019 with the Greek publishing house Vakxikon, and in the same year by the Centre for Slovenian Literature. Elsewhere, his poems have been published and translated into over ten languages. Currently, he is living between Ljubljana, Berlin, Prague, and Lisbon. To the first he returns to Slovene literature and to organize the International Critics' Symposium *The Art of Criticism*, in the second he prepares an anthology of young Slovene literature, in the third he is the program director of the International Literary Festival Microfestival, and in the last he often teaches at the Faculdade de Letras.

Polchate (Jam) Kraprayoon is a Bangkok native and now works for an intergovernmental agency in Tokyo. He received a Master's from the University of Oxford and a Bachelor's at the LSE. His work has been featured in *Glass: A Journal of Poetry, Harbor Review, Meniscus,* and *Portland Review*. He writes poems when he should really be writing policy briefs.

Taylor Mignon is an Outreach Editor of *RHINO: The Poetry Forum*. His essay "On the Road of the Beats in Japan" first appeared in *Tokyo Poetry Journal* Vol. 5, and has been republished by *Asymptote*. With electronic outfit Nw Nrml, his voice appears covering the song "In Heaven" (from the film *Eraserhead*). He has more collaborative poetry upcoming in *Sink Journal,* an experimental publication of poetry and criticism. Occasionally, his book reviews appear on *Kyoto Journal* online.

Richard Milner is a New York-born, Tokyo-based author, journalist, university English professor, and recovering video game narrative designer. He graduated with an MA in Digital Creative Media from Southern Methodist University, and BA in Psychology from Western Connecticut State University. Among others, he has written for *Rabbit Hole Magazine, Metropolis, Voyapon, the Japanese National Tourism Agency*, and various entertainment outlets. He recently accepted writing residencies in Finland and Spain for his latest, full-length experimental novel.

Onishi Takashi 大西高志 was born in Wakayama Prefecture in 1978. In this era of diversification and individualized values, his works aim to present simultaneously a universal familiarity of Japanese aesthetics, as well as aspects of modernity and reinvention. Currently, he exhibits his work around Japan and abroad, and serves as General Director of the Kudoyama Art Festival in Kudoyama, Wakayama Prefecture. rinto.main.jp

Oshima Takeo 大島健夫 is a poet from Chiba Prefecture, born in 1974. In 2014, he completed the world's first twenty-four hour one-man poetry reading performance. In 2016, he won the Poetry Slam Japan competition, and went on to the Poetry Slam World Cup in Paris, where he advanced to the semifinals. He has performed at international poetry festivals in Belgium, Israel, and Canada, and is featured in various poetry collections. He hosts a variety of long-running poetry performance events such as Chiba Poetry Pavilion (千葉詩亭). His program Poetry with You is delivered every Tuesday at 10 P.M. JST.

Photographer and graphic designer **Inka Piironen** comes from the cold Nordic, Finland. She has acted as photographer for several of TPJ's events during her exchange year. By the end of 2020, she will finish her studies and have a Bachelor's in Media. Inka wishes to return to Japan, and work as a producer or creative director some day in the future.

Alan Price lives in London. He is a poet, scriptwriter, short story writer, and film critic. His stories have been broadcast on Radio 3 and his TV film, *A Box of Swan*, was broadcast on BBC2. Alan's debut collection of poetry, *Outfoxing Hyenas*, was published in 2012. The poetry collection *Wardrobe Blues for a Japanese Lady* was published in 2018. Alan's collection of flash fiction, *The Illiterate Ghost*, appeared in November 2019. A book of cut-up poems etc., *Restless Voices* (Caparison Books), was published in February 2020, and *The Trio Confessions* (a volume of translations) came out this June.

Barbara Roether is a novelist and poet in North Carolina. Her most recent book is *Saraswati's Lament* (Wet Cement Press). She is also the author of the novel *This Earth You'll Come Back To* (McPherson & Company) and the poetry collection *The Middle Atlas*. She frequently reviews books, writes about the arts, and works whenever she can in Tokyo. www.barbararoether.com.

Eugene Ryan has been teaching English in Japan for twenty years, and now teaches at a university in Aichi, where he also manages international programs. His research interest is currently focused on using role playing games to help autistic children improve their communicative confidence. His poetry has been previously published in *Rat's Ass Review* and *The Font*.

Sasa/Marie is a sign language poet, spinning poetry through intertwined semiotic systems. Leader of the poetry and performance collective Denchuu gumi. Inhabitant of the liminal space between the non-hearing and the hearing. Mainly performs with Denchuu gumi members in antique houses, cafes, and live music houses, blending spoken and embodied language with music and full sensory experiences through poetry installations. Performed at Ueno Poetrican Jam 2017 and was selected for an art museum performance exhibition for Art Project TURN Fest 4 in 2018.

Jason Scuderi is a hybrid Visual and Commercial Artist living and working in Japan. As an award-winning Art and Creative Director, he has been an integral contributor for advertising and design agencies, architectural and development firms, and lifestyle consumer brands. Instagram @jasonscuderi

Xiao Yue Shan is a poet and editor born in China and based in Tokyo, Japan. Her chapbook, *How Often I Have Chosen Love*, was published in the spring of 2019. Find her at shellyshan.com.

Todd Silverstein regrets being carbon-based given the existence of elements like Yttrium and Flerovium on the periodic table. In addition to writing poetry, he's been a consulting producer on *Silicon Valley*, a ditch-digger, book editor with HarperCollins, dishwasher, and has twice been mistaken for Rivers Cuomo (he doesn't see it). Todd currently resides in Tokyo.

Durell Smith is an Edmonton, Canada-based poet writing on the anxieties and frustrations of everyday life. Accepting negativity and using it for fire. He frequently performs readings with drone, harsh noise, or ambient musical accompaniment, and is a curator of the Drone & Words performance series. His website is linktr.ee/DurellSmith.

Jordan A. Y. Smith writes, translates, professes, researches, curates, and produces performance-oriented events, mostly in Tokyo. Associate Professor of literature/translation at Josai International University, Creator/Partner at Technology Humans And Taste (Japan), Language Branding Director at TETE. Translations include that of Yoshimasu Gōzō, Furukawa Hideo, Saihate Tahi, Mizuta Noriko, Misumi Mizuki, Fuzuki Yumi, Michiyama Rain, and Sakisaka Kujira. Author of the poetry collection *Syzygy* (Awai Books 2020) and co-author of *Sea of Trees: Poetic Gateways to Aokigahara* (2019) and *√IC: Redux* (with Kanie Naha and Nagae Yūki). Founded of KOTOBA Slam Japan with Miki Yuuri. Two-time National Finalist in Poetry Slam Japan, and producer of BBC Radio 4 programs on Japanese poetry. @jordangiraffe on Instagram.

John Solt, poet, editor, and publisher, is a specialist and translator of Edo and modern Japanese art and literature. Recent publications include his translation of "The Poetic Competition of the Twelve Zodiac Animals" in *A Kamigata Anthology: Literature from Japan's Metropolitan Centers, 1600–1750*. His book *Poems for the Unborn* was translated by Aoki Eiko and published bilingually (Shichōsha, 2020). A selection of his recent poems, "Transcribed from Butterfly Wings," appeared in the August 2020 edition of *Gendai shi techō*, pp. 148–155.

Keijiro Suga 管啓次郎 is a poet and professor of critical theory in the graduate program Places, Arts, and Consciousness at Meiji University. Author of seven collections of poetry in Japanese and a chapbook in English, *Transit Blues*, he has been invited to read at poetry festivals and universities in over fifteen countries. He is also a prolific translator from English. French, and Spanish to Japanese. His most recent translation is Edouard Glissant's *Le quatrième siècle* (2019).

Leah Ann Sullivan's poetry has been published in *Modern Haiku*, *bottlerockets*, and *Sunrise over Blue Thunder*, an anthology of writing from the 2011 Tsunami. She was the founder and producer of the 1990s Nagoya Writers Group Open Reading Series. She performed spoken word with the music, art, and dance collectives 20-Squared and Expression Pow-Wow, as well as at Taylor Mignon's Collaborators retrospective.

Barbara Summerhawk edited *Sparkling Rain: And Other Fiction from Japan of Women Who Love Women* (2009) with Kim Hughes and is one of the founders of *Tokyo Poetry Journal*. She lives her life, for the most part, in longhand on the Wild West side of the Kanto plain.

Spencer Thurlow is the current Poet Laureate of West Tisbury, Massachusetts, USA, where he leads community readings, workshops, and more. His poetry or translations have appeared in *World Literature Today*, *Cincinnati Review*, *The Comstock Review*, and others.

K.V. Twain, real name Diana Carligeanu, was born in 1981 and is a bilingual Romanian writer educated in the US, the UK, and Japan (Waseda University, where she spent a semester). She has published a novella (*My Life with Salvador Dalí, by Babou the Ocelot*) and a poetry volume (*Not Playing God*), and has had poetry published in literary magazines from the US, the UK, Romania, and Germany. She has translated some of the works of Wallace Stevens, and is a translator into English of Mihai Eminescu's poetic oeuvre. Her first novel is in the works. She remains fond of the Japanese language and culture, which she studied for many years.

Joy Waller is a Canadian writer and editor based in Tokyo. She is the author of a poetry collection, *Pause :: Heartbeat* (2019 ToPoJo Excursions), and her short fiction and poetry have appeared in *The Fiddlehead Review*, *The Tokyo Poetry Journal*, *SAND*, *The Malahat Review*, and others.

Carl Walsh is an occasional poet, crossword compiler, lexicographer of fictional words and writer of horoscopes (and other fairytales). His work has been published in Australian and international journals including *n-SCRIBE*, *StylusLit*, *Australian Poetry Journal*, *Plumwood Mountain*, *Cordite*, *Rabbit*, *Southerly*, *Verity La*, *Meanjin*, *Cha: An Asian Literary Journal* (Hong Kong), *Takahe* (NZ), and *Wales Haiku Journal* (UK). In 2018, he visited Japan and can't wait to come back again. In the meantime, he's sustaining himself with translations of Mishima, Sōseki, Akutagawa, and Tanizaki...

Yoshida Kyoko 吉田恭子 was born and raised in Fukuoka, studied in Kyoto and Milwaukee, taught in Yokohama and Tokyo, and now teaches in Kyoto. She writes fiction in English and translates from/ into Japanese. Her story collection is *Disorientalism* (Vagabond Press), and her stories appear in BooksActually's *Gold Standard 2016* (Math Paper Press), *After Coetzee: An Anthology of Animal Fictions* (Faunary Press), and *Spring Sleepers* (Strangers Press). She is one of the co-translators of Yoshimasu Gōzō's *Alice Iris Red Horse*.